THE BOOKSHOP AT
10 CURZON STREET

*Letters between Nancy Mitford
and Heywood Hill 1952–73*

THE BOOKSHOP AT 10 CURZON STREET

*Letters between Nancy Mitford
and Heywood Hill 1952–73*

EDITED BY JOHN SAUMAREZ SMITH

FRANCES LINCOLN

THE BOOKSHOP AT 10 CURZON STREET

Frances Lincoln Limited
4 Torriano Mews
Torriano Avenue
London NW5 2RZ
www.franceslincoln.com

First Frances Lincoln edition: 2004

ISBN 0 7112 2452 8

Printed in England by St Edmundsbury Press

9 8 7 6 5 4 3 2 1

CONTENTS

INTRODUCTION

Nancy Mitford came to work in Heywood Hill's bookshop in March 1942. Between then and her death in 1973 she wrote letters to him, three hundred of which survive; they are the core of this book, selected for their entertainment value and timed to coincide with the centenary of her birth in 1904. Heywood wrote as regularly to her, but she did not keep those letters, with a single exception, until 1952. I have therefore summarised the period of the correspondence that covers the first ten years. Thereafter it is easier to work out what is missing and to get the flavour of their two-way affection.

Nancy Mitford's letters have been published in two collections, *Love From Nancy* (1993), and *The Letters of Nancy Mitford and Evelyn Waugh* (1996), both admirably edited by Charlotte Mosley. They give a cheerful, often hilarious, picture of her lives in London and Paris, with an editorial balance kept between the social and literary elements. This present selection has no biographical purpose to tell the events of her life through her letters; it concentrates on the relationship she had with a bookshop and its owner. When she worked there, she was under extraordinary pressure but she very much enjoyed the experience. Without her the business might well have failed in the latter years of the Second World War. When the war was over, she published *The Pursuit of Love* (1945), and its success enabled her to leave London and settle in Paris. But, like many of the bookshop's expatriate customers, she kept in touch with Heywood Hill and his colleagues. Heywood kept most of her letters. His colleagues did the same, but have since sold them at auction during the last few years. The story of the shop's evolution is therefore told through Heywood's eyes and is necessarily partisan. The letters make oblique reference to a simmering row between the Hills and the Buchanans, who also worked in the shop, but Nancy wanted no part in it and remained good friends with both parties. The dispute was unknown to all but a handful of the shop's customers.

Although I have been at 10 Curzon Street all my working life, I remember only one visit from Nancy. By chance she coincided with Harold Acton and they exchanged animated gossip in the children's room downstairs. She did write business letters to the shop and, when Heywood retired, there was competition between Handy and Mollie Buchanan and Miss Liz (Elizabeth Forbes) over who should read her letters first. The sorting of each morning's post was something of a ceremony, with Handy separating the brown envelopes and obvious bills from anything that looked hand-written and interesting. Any letter from Nancy would be carefully reserved on one side until he could pay full attention to it. He might then store it in an inside pocket or quote some of the better jokes to the rest of us; often, as her surviving friends would agree, they made their audience laugh aloud.

Many of Heywood's letters appeared in *Love From Nancy*. Harold Acton read them and quoted from them extensively in *Nancy Mitford: A Memoir* (1975). It would be a pity to omit everything that he chose, but a very large percentage of this selection is new. Some readers will know *A Bookseller's War* (1997), the letters between Heywood and his wife Anne while he was being trained as a soldier. He would have been the first to admit that this was a miserable period of his life. In the letters in this volume he reveals much more of his delightful character – charming, funny and gentle – which all his surviving friends and relations remember so well.

Heywood had learned about the book trade from the antiquarian dealer Charles Sawyer in Grafton Street. He served as an apprentice from 1929 to 1936, paying his employer for the experience. His father then lent him £2,000 and he opened his own shop at 17 Curzon Street in August 1936. Anne Gathorne-Hardy, only daughter of the 3rd Earl of Cranbrook, helped him in the shop and they employed a packer, Jim McKillop, in the basement. Both he and Anne described these early days in *A Bookseller's War*: the small scale of the business; the harshness of the 1930s that led to Elkin Mathews, a distinguished London bookshop, closing after fifty years; the unusual combination of their stock, not only books and prints, but children's games and musical boxes; and their marriage in 1938.

Meanwhile Handasyde Buchanan was working in another bookshop, Michael Williams, at 3 Curzon Street. He was the same age as Heywood and is best known for the reference books he wrote or part-wrote: *Fine Bird Books, Great Flower Books, Thornton's Temple of Flora* and *Nature Into Art*. When his shop was bombed in June 1940, he was recruited into press censorship and did not return to bookselling until 1945, when Heywood, not yet demobbed, asked him to become his partner in the business, which by then had moved down the road to 10 Curzon Street. Anne Hill had played a part in the shop when Heywood was first called up, but left in early 1943 to have her first baby. From then until 1945, the shop was run by Nancy Mitford, with considerable help from Mollie Friese-Green who did the accounts.

For details of Nancy's life, readers have a choice: Harold Acton's affectionate memoir, published soon after her death; Selina Hastings's sympathetic biography, published in 1985, and Laura Thompson's lively *Life in a Cold Climate* of 2003. There is no shortage of material on the Mitford family, from Jonathan Guinness's *The House of Mitford* (1984) to Mary Lovell's *The Mitford Girls* (2001).

Heywood's details are less familiar. He was born in 1907, went to Eton and, after a year at Cambridge, had a brief and unsuccessful career in the City. His school contemporaries included James Lees-Milne, Cyril Connolly, Harold Acton, Henry Yorke, Anthony Powell, Alan Pryce-Jones and Brian Howard. Many of them, plus others of that gifted literary generation, became customers of the shop in its early days: there are several accounts of shop meetings in the diaries of the time. In 1935 Anne Gathorne-Hardy had been engaged for three months to James Lees-Milne. Two of her older brothers, Eddie and Bob, worked for Elkin Mathews, and in the 1930s Bob acted as secretary-companion to Logan Pearsall Smith.

Nancy's letters are all written in her clear, legible longhand. She wrote the majority from her flat in Paris at 7 rue Monsieur, and after 1967 from 4 rue d'Artois, Versailles. When she went on holiday, I have shortened the addresses to, for example, Château de St Pierre, or simply Venice, but in all other cases the addresses can be assumed to be Paris. Luckily most letters are dated and, when they are headed "Sunday" or "Friday", the contents usually provide clues to the year, if not the month or week.

The originals of her letters are in the Hill archive in the Lilly Library at the University of Indiana. Photocopies were made of them to join the enormous letter archive at Chatsworth, and I have worked from a further set of photocopies which was provided by Nancy's sister and literary executor, the Dowager Duchess of Devonshire. While editing and transcribing the letters I was given wonderful encouragement: without her help and that of Helen Marchant at Chatsworth, I could never have finished this work within the time available.

Heywood's side of the correspondence went to the Chatsworth archive after Nancy's death. Until 1966 his letters were almost invariably typed from 10 Curzon Street. He used to describe his handwriting as "palsied" but on the rare occasions when he had no typewriter it is relatively easy to read. When working full-time he was constrained from writing at length by a busy shop. The letters expanded only when he retired and we hear more of his life at home and about his family and many friends. This may be a suitable time to mention my discovery that his later letters, to my considerable surprise, contain long quotations from the letters I was sending him during my first years in the bookshop. When he retired, I had asked him if he would like to know about occasional incidents, particularly if they were amusing, but he never mentioned that chunks were being copied out for Nancy. These extracts make for some pungent reading but are not included here – in an exchange of letters two voices are quite enough and a third would be a distraction.

In March 1970 Nancy wrote in a letter to her friend Lady Mersey, "A wonder post this morning – all the loved ones – you, Alphy [Prince Clary], Decca, Woman and Heywood Hill (whose letters, you know, beat all for funniness)". Funny they certainly are, but they are also witty, mischievous and affectionate, a rare combination. I have had the greatest pleasure in editing such an exchange and would like readers to share that pleasure.

John Saumarez Smith
June 2004

NOTE TO THE READER

To help readers, I have compiled a biographical index of the main characters mentioned in the letters (see page 182); this is indicated by an asterisk in the text where the character appears for the first time. Otherwise, there are short footnotes, but I hope they do not impede the epistolary flow.

I have omitted the tops and tails of the letters because they stayed consistently the same: "Dear Heywood" or "My dear Heywood" / "Love from Nancy" and "Dear Nancy" / "Love from Heywood".

Two words with special meaning survive from Nancy's days as a bookseller: "couch" for pile, sometimes adapted as "to couch" for "to put in a pile"; and "Gov" which means American. The latter derived from a remark made by Anne Hill to Nancy about Americans being "like governesses" (see letter of 1/10/71); Nancy never travelled in America and aired her prejudices when the Hills made plans to spend several months there in 1970 (see letter of 18/5/70).

There is no obvious consistency in either writer's use of French accents or style for the titles of books.

Nancy's first surviving letter dates from August 1942. "I had a smart set to with Evelyn about the marmalade cat having gone up to 6/s; however in the end he took it . . . A terrific tart has just been in to ask if you are Mr Hill from Valparaiso – well, really Heywood . . . Please tell me how much are the new shell (china) pair of ornaments on the mantle piece in the lit room? Mrs Macleod wants them. (Hope you don't mind this flow of dirt. If it ruins your hol just tell me and I'll stop.)" By the second letter Heywood has been called up. This happened just before Christmas and, from the letters presented in *Bookseller's War*, the first few days were chaotic. "You would be amazed," wrote Nancy on New Year's Eve, "at the horror wrought in the shelves – almost a bore as there is hardly anything to show people or make traps with! . . . Anne's glamorous brother [Bob?] has just asked me out to lunch so I must let up a bit."

Unfortunately no further letters survive from this wartime period except a relatively serious one written in October 1944 about Nancy's future role in the bookshop. Heywood must have suggested some sort of partnership once he was demobbed, but Nancy did not want to commit herself: the whole letter, complete with an account of a buying expedition to Brown's Antiquarian Bookshop in Eton, is reproduced in *Love from Nancy*.

By July 1945 she was clearer about her plans. "I have been given £5000 to start a business with. Do you want my money, would you like to have me as a partner? I can't work full time any more but could probably do 3 days a week or every morning, or afternoon, as fits in best with the arrangements of others. I want to concentrate really on the import and export side which I shall know more about when I have been to Paris. I suppose the question is, can the firm cope with any more business – probably not unless a full-time accountant was engaged . . . . It suits me to sell [French books] through the shop better than to start off in a new place. I'll put up all the money so that if it flops you won't be out of pocket . . . it really seems sensible to combine." After finding a flat in Paris, Nancy handed over £3,000 to Heywood's business as her share of the shop's capital. It led to misunderstandings over a long period. In March 1948 she received a letter from a solicitor in which she was told that no dividend would be paid on her share. She wanted this to be sorted out at an annual meeting. "Needless to say nobody has thought of consulting me since the ill-considered words were spoken. What now? I don't at all want to deal out three body blows [presumably to Heywood, Handy and Mollie] . . .; perhaps someone cleverer than me ought to go to [the meeting] because I must confess I sit in an utter fog throughout. Oh *business* – how can people?"

By May 1948 it seems as if Edwin, her lawyer, had made peace and that she would accept a dividend of £150: she told him to "call off his clockwork mouse". A few days later she wrote to Heywood: "I think doing business with friends is impossible and makes things too disagreeable for both sides . . . Best love – *do* let's have a divorce."

Despite these upsets Nancy continued to correspond regularly and to buy both old and new books from the shop. She always came to the shop when she visited London and encouraged Heywood to stay with her when he went to Paris. This was partly due to the restrictions on how much money could then be taken out of England. Her letters refer to problems with the Treasury. In October 1949: "I've been waiting a fortnight for the typescript of my Princesse [de Cleves]," which she had sent to be typed by a friend in Oxfordshire, "&, can you beat it, the Treasury have now sequestered it wanting to know how much I pay to have it done. They do make life a treat, don't they?"

As a customer she wanted to send copies of her novels to friends in France. She also needed exercise books from Rymans in which she wrote her novels, and solander boxes specially made and monogrammed by Mr Hobson at Sangorski and Sutcliffe. She took considerable trouble over the design of these boxes, often involving her emblem of a mole in gilt patterns. She was delighted when they turned out very handsome.

As a partner of the shop she recommended books that were having a success in Paris and might be worth stocking by Heywood. She also alerted him to illustrated books such as her favourite Grandvilles (*Les Fleurs Animées*, etc.) which turned up in Paris quite often; when Heywood did not respond to her enthusiasm in 1947, she bought the Grandvilles for herself.

Nancy naturally wanted to hear that the shop praised her own novels. "I'm so relieved you like the book," she told him in November 1949. "After the drubbing I had from Evelyn [Waugh] and Christopher [Sykes] & the gloom from Handy ("very uneven, I fear") it is the greatest comfort if you and Anne whom I believe in, liked it." In May 1951 Heywood was sent an early proof of *The Blessing*. In response to his letter, she wrote, "I'm so delighted you like The Blessing, enjoyed your letter about it very much."

During the summer of 1950 Nancy went to Scotland for a production of *The Little Hut*.[1] This was directed by Peter

---

1. André Roussin's farce, *La Petite Hutte*, had first been produced in 1947 to great success. N.M.'s translation of it was published in 1951.

Brook whom she described as "an angel & a human being". She was not so keen on the actors: she quoted them as saying "Sorry, you know but I can't say that line" or complaining, "What about MY EXIT?"

The letters contain plenty of gossip about Paris and her English friends there. Without a multitude of footnotes it is not easy to pick up on their shared in-jokes: what would a modern reader make of her description of "Derek Hill as literally Helen Dashwood in trousers"? She was often surprised by the attitude of English visitors in Paris. "I believe they think that Paris is a social desert where nobody knows anybody else and sits waiting for visitors to cheer them up. Like some little port in the Red Sea." And she made jokes at her own expense: "Just off to dine chez Windsor in a terrible fix as it is *tenue de ville* i.e. jewelled jacket costing £600 which I do *not* possess. All my horrid clothes are laid out like a jumble sale & I in tears! . . . As I write these words, the secretary rang up & said it's short evening dresses . . ."

She could get into trouble with her teases. In October 1949 Gilbert Fabes, a second-hand bookseller in Rye, ticked her off for "throwing mud at booksellers who try to serve their customers well." "Isn't this awful?" she scribbled at the bottom: "I've written a *grovel* saying I was a bookseller too & I do see I've been a brute but all *meant* to be *funny*." Mr Fabes was mollified and sent her a recent catalogue of his books: "glorious because he seems to have all Henry James's books so I've ordered like mad from it." In the same letter, she added later that "of course they've all been sold & the one I wanted least is coming. Typical."

Once *The Blessing* had been corrected in typescript, she asked Heywood to put it in a taxi and rush it up to Hamish Hamilton (Jamie). He is "in the usual wild hurry". From then until August 1951 when it was published, Nancy wrote regularly, particularly in the month of July when she was staying in the south of France with Tony Gandarillas.[2] In one week she had had "a bitter blow – been offered 100,000 dollars for a film [of *The Blessing*], but am obliged to sell it to Korda for £3000 as it was his idea (just the child was, nothing else) . . . quite a swiz."[3]

Three longer quotations from her letters give a better flavour than scraps, the first from 31 October 1949:

Merino [a book runner[4]] & wife lunched here & brought me a lovely present, Memoires of Mme de Caylus . . . Both he & his wife called me Nancy which I am all for, only what am I expected to call them? It's like with Mr Maugham who calls me Nancy & I always feel I can't get out Willie . . . Oh for an amusing novel – no not Henry Green [much admired by H.H.], not yet at least. How I wish I could get on with Miss Compton Burnett [a close friend of H.H.] but it's my blind spot. So I plod on with St. Simon, such a nice readable edition, Racine, which, on account of the notes, is as good as Punch.

Then, five weeks later:

Diana [Mosley] is here, she says she will have to walk barefoot to Curzon Street when she gets back and explain all to Handy. She said when she was thinking the worst [about the bookshop not supporting a book she was publishing at the Euphorion Press], my mother (who always takes sides wildly, you know) said "Do you know of a good bookshop?" To which D. replied "Well, there's Truslove & H[anson]," upon this a bellow from

---

2. Tony Gandarillas (d. 1970), Chilean diplomat.

3. *Count Your Blessings* eventually appeared in 1959 with Maurice Chevalier as the Duc de St Cloud.

4. Book runners made a living by buying books from provincial shops and re-selling them in London's West End.

Mogens[5] in the next room "Vot is thees? Every VORD goes back to Nancy" Rather wonderful & loyal?

The third is undated but clearly coincides with Nancy's early chapters of *The Blessing* (late 1950):

Am I right in thinking that an uncle can take a boy out [from Eton] on Sunday? [She wanted to get the details right about the time of the boys' dinner]. May I say tickets for this (highbrow) theatre were obtainable at Heywood Hill's and make one of the characters ring you up for a copy of L[ittle] L[ord] F[auntleroy]?

I've got Cyril [Connolly] to the life I think. He runs this theatre called The Royal George & all those girls are the crew and he is the Captain & he courts the rich heroine & the crew are furious & finally when he tries to put on Little L.F. instead of a modern Finnish play they mutiny.

PS Do scribble the names of one or 2 tremendously highbrow Horizon – Penguin N[ew] W[riting] writers – I can only think of Capetenakis and he's dead so it seems rather poor taste . . . Also if you could think of an intensely dreary play for them to have in their repertory . . .

That takes us, at a gallop, to the end of 1951.

---

5. Mogens Tvede (1897–1977), Danish painter and architect; husband of Princess Dolly Radziwill.

1952

N.M.   9/1/52   7 rue Monsieur, Paris.

. . . I jotted down particulars of a very pretty book in green morocco & apparently perfect state.

R.P. Lesson   Hist: Nat: des Oiseaux Mouches 1829.
85 very very pretty plates, life size, 8vo green morocco, 15,000 francs. Just in case. I could bring it if you like.

. . . Have I boasted about the 200 Gov: women ("all keen Mitford fans") who are giving a luncheon for me next Monday? I only hope it's not to beat me up. Evangeline Bruce[6] the ambassadress is very giggly about it, I note. . . .

N.M.   22/1/52

My life has been terrible – trop de dîners en ville – & I'm cross, fractious, haven't read a word even N[ew] S[tatesman] for days & in short it doesn't suit me. This week I've chucked everything & life is beginning to be possible once more. . . . 200 Gov: ladies gave a luncheon for me & I was introduced as "one of Doctor Redesdale's 6 daughters". Luckily there was no eye to catch. . . .

I've made £10,000 last year; not bad is it, but I need more so that I can go out hunting, it's all I think of now . . .

N.M.   1/2/52

. . . I went to a terrible dinner to meet Mlle Yourcenaar.[7] All

6. Evangeline Bruce (1914–95), wife of David Bruce, U.S. Ambassador in Paris and later in London.
7. Marguerite Yourcenaar (1903–88), author of *Memoirs of Hadrian* and member of the French Academy.

but me were drugged to the eyes & clearly orgies were about
to take place – prim & English, I fled . . .

Can I have please

Ch. Oman: English Silver from Charles II pub. Connois-
sueur 3/6 if not a bore.

In a letter that has disappeared N.M. *suggested that an
impoverished friend of hers, Jacques Brousse, might come
to London a few weeks later to translate* Look Down in
Mercy *by Walter Baxter (1951) and stay for a few days as a
paying guest with the Hills in Maida Vale. Heywood agreed,
in a letter that has also vanished, and referred to Brousse
as Hysterico.*

N.M.   19/2/52

. . . Hysterico PERFECT only it must be at least £1 otherwise you'll lose. He won't stay more than 4 or 5 days I'm sure.
I *think* he's more piercingly hysterical with me because of
slight love – always so tiresome when women say that, but I
think so. Tho' he may be queer I wouldn't be sure. . . . I'll tell
Hysterico you've offered – really it is kind.

N.M.   3/3/52

. . . Oh I did have a lovely gossip with H[amish] H[amil-
ton]'s sales manager. I made poor Jamie [Hamilton] send him
by complaining once a week that nobody can get my books
here. Jamie's reply always was the booksellers must be telling
lies, but finally the mystery is unravelled – hundreds of Blessings are lying at the Customs. . . .

H.H.   7/3/52

. . . I had a good laugh about your lèse-majesté, treason and
irreverence. The whole thing was of course immensely over-

done in the Press. [King George VI had died in February.] And then, in a subtle way, the mourning business has become a sort of snob and class thing. You know I suppose that the right people are wearing black until May (and if you are VERY right, a fur coat doesn't count). The row of pearls and regimental brooch show up splendidly. Anne & I have been immensely irreverent and we haven't been able to be right people as we haven't any black & will not go and dye ourselves. There's a huge lot of humbug and suburban shintoism which swamps the original sad fact. People were genuinely shocked at first but surely they cannot still be. . . .

N.M.   9/3/52

Hysterico in a great state because somebody NOT ME has told him that if you allow food to pass your lips in London you die poisoned. So he wants to be allowed to *boil potatoes* (which he will take with him) in Anne's kitchen!! I was most discouraging & if you can't face it all I will *get you* out *of it in a jiffy*. I must say that I laughed so terribly that I don't think he saw how much put out I was . . . He keeps saying he can't afford food poisoning & yet must eat something, if he is to go round seeing the sights, to keep up his strength. He asked if you were lettré – he expects all the English to be hopelessly uncultured like me (he can't even get over the horror of my barbaric ignorance – I think being a schoolmaster has had an effect on his outlook). When I said you were, very, he looked greatly relieved. . . .

Talking of difficult, Evelyn [Waugh] has eaten up my week. He says you & he *love* each other now. I must admit he was most unexpectedly nice & jolly with my great new friend John Russell,[8] who told us some lovely things about the Captain [Cyril Connolly]. Do you, by the way, think that the

8. John Russell (b. 1919), art historian and distinguished journalist.

Captain is cross with me & should I send him a small peace offering? What do you advise? I suddenly remembered how much, really, I love him, on hearing things like his favourite daydream which is that he is a great pianist & if people hear him playing as they walk in the street (by chance) they look at each other & say "that can only be Connolly". . . .

I thought of coming [to London] for a day or 2 in April but as I've nothing black or even brown (all red & blue) I suppose I should be lynched. What rubbish – I didn't wear black for Tom or Bobo.[9]

H.H.   12/3/52

Anne & I were so armoured by your first description of Hysterico that his first request to Anne if she "would not mind me to cook rice and potatoes in her kitchen every day, I know I could manage well enough with what I could bring from here to be able to visit London a little" seemed nothing at all. Though I must say that I had to have three drinks before "approaching" Mary the cook who is the person who matters of course. I read her the letter & it made her laugh too and all was well and she said she was sure she would rather that Mr. Brush should cook for himself than she should cook for him. . . . You mustn't get nervo-hysterico yourself about it all or think that it is going to be like one of those avalanches of mud and horror (rice and potatoes) which one is inclined to start by pushing a pea. Anne & I can take, and have taken, a great deal, and shall be expecting piles of burnt-out saucepans and rice splashed all over the kitchen floor.

I am only rather appalled that you have told him that I am very lettré. I don't consider myself any more lettré than you. Much better to let him go on thinking that we are all fearful savages and then he might sometimes have a tiny surprise.

9. N.M.'s only brother Tom (1909–45) and her sister Unity (1914–48).

Handy has been laughing at me because Madame Romain Gary (L. Blanch)[10] wrote & asked me for an animal print she had seen here. She described it as a picture of "some beavers tusking away at a dam". I thought a dam must mean a woman beaver and was vaguely surprised at Mme. Gary's unusual frankness – but of course, she only meant a water dam.

N.M.   13/3/52

Oh I'm dead to the world after taking Mr. Brush to Dior, a long promised treat (for him). He arrived in a scream of "I am saved. A friend has just come from London & tells me that boiled vegetables & even my dear *boiled fish* are *quite easy* to get there." . . . When you go away he is going to find himself a cheap room in the quartier Latin. . . . Then his friend has told him you can quite easily get bread. "But my dear how could I have guessed that – I know you don't grow wheat in England." . . . Goodness he is tiring. I feel as if I'd been put through a sieve & the maddening thing is he knows it himself & yet takes no steps such as going away after one has had him rushing around (quite chastely like Leslie [Hartley][11]) for 7 hours or so.

N.M.   21/3/52

Oh I begin to feel worried. I'm so afraid he will wear you out. Only, as he is very delicate I'm in hopes that London will wear him out first. You must defend yourself tooth & nail.

N.M.   27/3/52

I feel in a fever – shan't really know another peaceful mo-

---

10. Lesley Blanch (b. 1907), illustrator and writer.
11. L. P. Hartley, novelist, best known for *The Go-Between* (1953).

ment until THE VISIT is over. But as you say you can take refuge in *work*. Luckily I know you like oddities as I do & know in a way he'll amuse you. I only fear the whole thing will be too intensive.

I've now very mischievously written to him "remember Heywood's wife is Lady Anne – you may call her Madame but the word Mrs. *must never* cross your lips. This I think will cause brain fever, because like all Frenchmen he is a monumental snob (He informed me the other day that he is descended from Robert the Bruce – but I'm afraid it's really the spider). . . .

Hysterico, who loves to take one down a few pegs, pronounced last time I saw him that the novels of *my* 2 friends L. P. Hartley & T. Powell are "exécrables".[12]

I *count* on you to tell me every penny of expenses – taxis, theatre, boiled fish & all the works. That will help to pacify my conscience a bit.

H.H.   30/3/52

Mrs Hammersley[13] came in this week in wonderfully sly & wicked form. There seemed to be more and thicker black net than ever hangin' all around. Why does she not carry a triton? She said that you had said she could have a book, and *did* I think Hugh Walpole too expensive (25/-)? I said NO & we both gave devilish chuckles. Then her eye fell on Dolly Wilde and, looking at me with that very sidelong look and her voice sinking even deeper, she said "would it, could it be possible that you would give her that too?" When I said yes we

---

12. L. P. Hartley's *My Fellow Devils* was published in 1951, as was a collection of short stories. The novel by Anthony Powell (1905–2000) might be *A Question of Upbringing* (1951).
13. Mrs Violet Hammersley (1877–1964), a widow whom N.M. mercilessly teased because of her innate pessimism.

lowered our heads in enjoyable shame & knew that we were linked in treacherous complicity.

Another letter from Hysterico yesterday saying I shall recognise him because he will be waving the newspaper "Le Monde". Perhaps I'd better bring a stirrup-pump to calm him down. He says that he feels the same about his visit as the hero of "Look Down" when he had to cross Burma on foot pursued by the Japanese. I'm writing to tell him that it's far more like Siberia now and that he must bring some wraps. Snow is thick and there are blizzards. . . .

Have you ever heard of a French caricaturist of the eighties or nineties called "Bob"? I got the other day through the Clique[14] a book by Gyp which was illustrated by him and I was bowled over by it. Funnier than Thurber, Lancaster or anyone . . .

N.M.   1/4/52

I forgive you. I have seen her doing the dance of the 7 veils to the butcher in T[otland] Bay as a result of which fatted calves lowed into her kitchen – *none* can resist her wiles.

Gaston[15] & I once took a train to the country in search of antiques. The antiquaire said his gardener would be at the station holding the Figaro & when we arrived we saw a man waving a fully opened Figaro up & down like a flag. We had such terrible giggles we had to get back in the train. But Hysterico will have lost Le Monde for sure & certain. You will know him by his terribly ill look, his wild hunted movements & a dark grey top coat, much too big for him, specially made for the Duke of Windsor's cocktail party.

---

14. A weekly magazine in which booksellers advertised their customers' wish lists.
15. Gaston Palewski ("Colonel") (1901–84), principal political adviser to de Gaulle in London and the great love of N.M.'s life.

H.H.   8/4/52

The train was one & a quarter hours late owing to the rough seas and the boat having to circle outside the harbour before it dared come into it. I was almost fainting with apprehension by the time the train did arrive & stood there in a brown tweed cap (which I said I would be recognised by) waiting to be assaulted by some gibbering gesticulating creature smelling of sick. There was nothing like that in view – not a sign of anyone jerking a newssheet up and down – and I was just resigning myself to another hour's wait when I heard a tiny voice say "Is it Mr. Hill?" Relief was enormous when he appeared to be more human than animal because I was really expecting some screaming monster freak; perhaps I felt also the tiniest tinge of disappointment. He was proud of himself because he had not been sick. He said that everyone else was prostrate. He must have helped to make them so because, as far as I can make out, he and "a beautiful English pederast" (I think he only *guessed* that) had gone round offering bananas to sick persons.

As we were going up Grosvenor Crescent in a taxi he asked if that was a "good quarter" and I said I thought it was but perhaps not so good as it used to be. He said how odd because in Paris none of the good quarters were near the main railway stations. He was delighted when I showed him the tub thumpers at Marble Arch. On getting to Warwick Av., the first thing he did was to unpack his fodder which consisted of butter, stale sandwiches, bananas and a stump of ham. He asked if the stale sandwiches could be put in a tin box so that he could eat them during the nights. He also asked if the butter here was pasteurisé, which is the sort of thing I never know but said yes. Mary & I were triumphant when he ate the dinner which we had thought out together. Vegetable soup (TINNED – but he never knew it), poached eggs, boiled potatoes and boiled cauliflower). We discussed "Looked Down in Mercy" at length and then speculated about the author who I say must be the hero personified. The great interest is to discover whether the man who lives with him is a batman. Also, if so, whether Baxter is the husband or the wife. I say wife but Hysterico, after talking to him on the telephone this morning, says husband because his voice is so deep. I say it doesn't follow at all. . . . He went to bed at 10.30 when I told him to – so the beginning, for me, was as good as could be. I enjoyed talking to him and liked him. He is as if made of matchstick – don't you think – and as if he would so easily break. He makes me feel very anxious about him and I did not like leaving him alone when I had to come here [the bookshop] this morning. I tried very hard to explain about taking a 16 [bus] down Edgware Road but did quite visualise all the enormous difficulties. He said that he didn't want to go to any museums and his plan was to go to Waterloo where he had read the effect was quite extraordinary if you went down the street to Waterloo Bridge, crossed over it and found yourself in the Strand. I said that I thought perhaps the effect might be better if he crossed Westminster Bridge but that he must not expect any enormous effect anyway. At that he laughed – it's a great saving thing his laugh, isn't it? He will have to carry his butter throughout the expedition as he is coming here to go out to luncheon with me. He might have to bring a banana too. I can't believe that he can ever possibly find here. . . .

N.M.   [? April '52; from Lismore Castle]

I am so grateful. I got a letter from him, the first day or so, saying he felt rather torn between waiting to be with you & thinking he must do whatever Baxter asked him to, & saying when I am with H., we laugh all the time.

N.M.   22/5/52

. . . It's a mercy the Blessing did so well as I haven't an idea in my head & could no more write a novel at the moment than fly.

During a short stay in London N.M. had thrown a party in Hamilton Terrace at the home of her publisher, to which "110 came, including many booksellers which I thought very cunning of me. Anyway I love them."

N.M.   1/6/52

Having just given a party myself, I do know the agony of the numbers & how they seem to double every time one looks at the list & have children, not to speak of the partners everyone wants to bring. . . .

Yes my oeuvre. *You wait.* "Miss M is experimenting, & though one cannot say it is entirely successful the result is not without interest." "Important new departure" and so on!

There's an awful new party-giver's menace here, do you have it? which is the chaps ring up & ask if they may bring their homosexual wives, "my friend" or "Hans who stays in my flat" or in one case "my partner" just like a deb. dance. They all did it to Schiap[arelli] last week & she wasn't having any but I'm so soft on the telephone & said yes yes. So one gets a crowd of these sub-normal gorillas who no doubt swing wonderfully but have no conversation at all & don't look pretty either (or anyway not to ONE).

N.M.   2/6/52

A long session with Jacques – at his very worst. Came in on a shriek of darling whereupon I saw red & said, very unkindly, you can't call me darling, it's not done in England. (Just like Diana Cooper who tu-toyers everybody, but the

French are nicer than I am & only laugh.) This got him into a state of frenzied nerves & I was sorry really for having snubbed him, & then he couldn't go & was here for nearly 2 hours. . . . By the way Jacques *adores* you. I said isn't the house nice & he said "oh *yes* it so reminded me of Danemark, all that comfort."

N.M.   9/6/52

. . . We've found a wonderful fortune teller or at least Debo told us (Diana & me) about her. She took one look at my hand & cried "Oh Madame, *comme* vous êtes heureuse dans votre situation!" which just exactly hits it off. . . .

Another bit of [cheese]paring is Hamishham[ilton] let me have new books at cost price – is it very disloyal of me? They are so dreadfully expensive & as you know I have to buy everything I read & can't belong to a library like most people. And then I can't read everything I buy – Doting[16] for example. . . .

N.M.   24/6/52

. . . My Sevigné is a dear little copy in nice old calf & belonged to Henry James. I got it out of a catalogue, I think. Yes, I ought to have yours of course but I think I won't. For one thing I've so little room for books you know. . . .

N.M.   23/8/52   Chateau de St. Pierre, Hyères, Var.

. . . I had an amusing drive down, 3 stops on the way, 2 French & Douglas Cooper & John Richardson.[17] They had a couple with a German name staying with them, I felt I should

---

16. Novel by Henry Green, published in 1952.
17. Douglas Cooper (1911–84), collector and art historian, and John Richardson (b. 1924), biographer of Picasso.

be able to place – she a blonde & either a friend or a relation (possibly sister) of Elizabeth Glenconner.[18] Who would that be? I detected a distinctly Heywood Hillish ambiance I thought in the talk. . . .

I must say the lists of new books are far from tempting. I rather long for George V but £2!![19] and I'm having an economy drive, can't be so carefree now the Hut is finishing.

N.M.   26/8/52   Hyères.

. . . Did I tell you I had a long fan letter ending up P.S. Are you THE Nancy Mitford? What could he have meant? Prize to whoever thinks up a likely answer. I was too shy to ask.

N.M.   7/9/52   Hyères.

. . . Fancy *Pigeon Pie* has had better notices in the US than any of my books – rather discouraging really. I believe people only want to laugh after all. I haven't had *Hemlock* yet[20] – though cheaper to get books by H. Hamilton it's certainly quicker via H. Hill. . . . *Pigeon Pie* will carry me over another year & then I must turn an honest penny or leave Paris.

N.M.   25/9/52

. . . You'll be amused to hear I had dinner on the train with 3 English – a man who had been selling boilers to Tito & a *sweet* bookseller & wife called Fletcher. I said I used to work for Mr. H.H.; they responded like mad & said you ought to go to Zagreb – pay your journey over & over again through a wonderful bookshop . . .

---

18. Elizabeth Glenconner (b. 1914). Her son, Toby Tennant, married Deborah Devonshire's daughter Lady Emma Cavendish in 1963.
19. Official biography by Harold Nicolson, published in 1952.
20. *Hemlock and After* by Angus Wilson, published in 1952.

N.M.   2/10/52

. . . My dear book friend has sent his catalogue – Preston &
Fletcher – & Preston seems to be the *town* where he lives, not
his name. Very muddling. He sent a lovely catalogue, 10% off
on account of having once worked with you. Did I tell you he
shook his head over your shop being so small until I
explained that the customers love being pressed bosom to
bosom . . .

N.M.   6/11/52

. . . I've been asked to send a short autobiographical sketch
of myself to a Gov. literary Who's Who. They send a sample:
"It was during the years of bitter poverty in the hut of old
Gabe the Trapper that the poet in me was born." I've said that
I was born in the slums of London because my father was a
second son – in England second sons are always poor. I
suggest that it was during the bitter years since he died that
the poet in *me* was born. Do tell Osbert [Sitwell].

*In a letter dated 11/11/52, unaccountably now missing, N.M.
told H.H. that she was to "do a life of Mme. de Pompadour".
"My difficulty is going to be bibliography . . . I must try & do
as little Bibliothèque Nationale as possible because my poor
old brain doesn't function much in such places."*

N.M.   14/11/52

. . . I shall soon be Norway's lodger I can see.[21] The Treasury have refused to count me as a foreign resident &
have nabbed ½ my earnings & the French Gov., who do so

---

21. Norway (Mrs Rusted) ran a small restaurant in Warwick Place. Both she
and the restaurant were nicknamed Norway.

count me, have nabbed the rest. Out of £7000 I am left with
£500 (for 1951). In 1952, which was a bit better, I may net
£700 . . .[22]

---

22. These figures, even if exaggerated, are hard to credit.

1953

Several letters of this period are devoted to N.M*'s research for* Madame de Pompadour. *She would ask* H.H. *to "clique"* The Fascinating Duc de Richelieu, *1908: "such heaven, he* loathed Pomp. *& thought of hundreds of ways to tease her".* *"Various kind people have given me a lot of lives in French, but the fact is it's much more amusing to go to the sources, most of which I have now got. . . ."*

N.M.   9/2/53

. . . I've just had an idea, which is to ask Francis Watson[23] if, for a fee, he would write a supplementary chapter on Pomp. & art. It's a huge subject & would take me weeks to mug it up – he has it at his fingertips. . . . Could you sell the Ms. of Blessing for a few pounds d' you think? It's quite clear.

N.M.   13/2/53

. . . Three days with a wet towel & I have mastered les parlements, feeling very smug about it. Perhaps one is not as stupid as ONE thinks in the end.

N.M.   26/2/53

. . . I do want a life of Voltaire but I don't believe such a thing exists. "Ah Madame," said a bookseller, "il s'est tellement expliqué lui-même," & offered me his works in some 40 vols. . . . I'm trying to join London Library simply because of

---

23. Francis Watson (1907–72), art historian and director of the Wallace Collection.

lack of space, but some say they don't send abroad old books in which case useless to me . . .

N.M.   15/4/53   Pension Maintenon, Versailles.

Getting on famously except that I'm tortured by my eyes which is a bore because if I can't write all day, or read, there's nothing I can do except sit with them shut & that is so dull when one's dying to be *at it*.

Could I have (cheapest possible) L. Strachey Q. Vic.?[24] I want to see the form, length, bibliography, & so on.

This place is sheerest heaven & will do in future instead of the country cottage I thought I must have. So far more convenient in every way. . . . The book is good I believe, coming on famously, & as for Versailles in the Spring it's quite indescribable.

N.M.   [4/53]

. . . The eyes are rotten. They vary curiously according to how interested I am & today I've had a *treat*, describing the battle of Fontenoy, & they never played up once.

Miss M. Trouncer[25] has been to the library here APPALLED that I'm doing it, furiously angry, says I must be mad, there's nothing more to say on the subject. I do love the way people think it's sufficient to slap down a lot of more or less correct facts on a cold plate, & that the public will then fall to with relish . . .

N.M.   24/6/53

. . . An American here has written a perfectly excellent little

24. Lytton Strachey's *Queen Victoria* was first published in 1921.
25. Margaret Trouncer, francophile biographer who later lived in Charles Street, near the bookshop.

book on how to buy French furniture & china, & published it
himself. He is doing very well with it (300 a day). I asked how
about London & he has made no arrangement – I believe it
would be quite a scoop if you could be the sole sellers of it, so
I've given him your name & address & he may go & see you.
This is just to warn you. The trouble is it's rather expensive –
sells at 700 francs.

N.M.   2/7/53

. . . I've got a luncheon party today. Violet [Trefusis][26]
arrived for it yesterday – I was eating a little bit of fish. I said
you *must* go away, but she tottered to the table, scooped up
all the fish & *all* the potatoes, left half & threw cigarette ash
over it. I could have killed her. Lady Montdore exactly.[27]

N.M.   18/7/53

. . . I gave Pomp to Hamisham (who came specially) in the
afternoon, & met him for dinner & *died* on the way there.
"I'm sure you'll easily find another publisher" was what I
envisaged, & only saying it after dinner when I felt stronger.
However one look at his face & could see all was well. The
relief was great.

N.M. needed to spend most of August in London because
The Little Hut *was going to be put on at a London theatre.
She did not want to stay in a hotel. H.H. asked if she would
like to stay at Warwick Avenue: "I'm not much trouble as
you know, no meals or hardly – just sometimes a little
ironing. I shall be in the theatre most of the time." She*

---

26. Violet Trefusis (1894–1972), novelist, celebrated for her affair with
Vita Sackville-West.
27. Memorable character in N.M.'s *Love in a Cold Climate*.

suggested "£10-10 a week, with Mary [who worked in the house]."

N.M.   8/8/53   10 Warwick Avenue

Just a single word to say NEVER have I been so happy & comfortable – it is saving my reason that's all because I can sleep here, so quiet & airy. Thankyou thankyou.

N.M.   9/9/53

. . . Evelyn writes to say that as a shareholder I ought to know that one of your assistants puts the customers off buying books (his). I feel entirely on the side of the assistant if he is referring to his latest effort [Men at Arms].

N.M.   29/12/53

. . . I've given a Courbet to Colonel for Xmas & to myself a chest of drawers for £250 so ruin is nigh. It's all on strength of Pomp being Book o' Month for March, did I tell you?

1954

N.M. 13/1/54

How can I resist the Louis XV silver book? Please send it. If Pompadour sells I'll be all right & if not the future is extremely bleak.

H.H. 27/1/54

. . . Harold Acton* dances more than usual for joy and relief because Brian Howard[28] declares that he has "settled" in Spain. Not for long, I guess. Harold complains of the exhaustion of late nights in London and the necessity of drinking spirits in order to get through them and of the queenly behaviour of Princess Marthe Bibesco[29] (My dear, she arrived two hours late and then Alan had to cook a little special supper for her and then I had to take her back to the Ritz and I did not get to bed until 2 o'clock. Oh, the TEDIUM!)

H.H. 4/2/54

I think you are over gloomy about Pomp's appearance. Cecil [Beaton]'s cover is maybe too fussy and vogueish and not really worthy – but it by no means looks at all a trashy book. The illustrations are lovely, the paper and print good, it opens well and it is nice to handle. I am not just trying to be soothing. I do see however how you must feel sensitive over a

28. Brian Howard (1905–58), exotic Anglo-American writer.
29. Princess Marthe Bibesco (1888–1973), novelist and writer, married to Prince Georges Bibesco.

child of such long delivery. Thankyou very much for my mention – which I was delighted to have.

N.M.   18/2/54

. . . Yes, I'd heard that you are being most loyal over Pomp. . . . What can I write now, that is the dreadful problem.

Jamie is upset because Cyril [Connolly] is going to do Pomp in the S. Times & Jamie says he's sure to carp. But I say even if he does carp his review will be so much more interesting than another's would be that I am all for it.

N.M.   27/2/54

You don't mention the beastly appearance of Pomp which has greatly modified my pleasure at seeing her in print . . . Also the Index, which I couldn't do myself, because of the usual silly haste, is a disaster. He tells me he has printed 50,000 – very nice for me, but no hope of any corrections I fear . . .

Two of N.M.'s letters to H.H. in March are reprinted in Love from Nancy. *She had problems over the book's distribution in Paris and W. H. Smith wanted her for a spectacular book signing. Several reviews had appeared, "the most beastly" by A. J. P. Taylor and a funny one by Cyril Connolly. The* Sunday Times *wanted her to write a weekly article.*

N.M.   18/3/54

. . . Tony Lambton[30] told my mother your shop is like an altar to Pompadour. How loyal. I do wish you could see W. H. Smith's window here. Nothing but Pomp, great nudes of her

---

30. Viscount Lambton (b. 1922), politician and biographer.

by Boucher & a dirty old black velvet hat with a feather. Poor Marquise. The dreadful signing day is tomorrow – I'm dying of fright. Will they make me wear the hat?

N.M.   22/3/54

. . . Oh the signing! Debo saw in Nice-Matin (she was down there) that it was to take place so she came straight from the aeroplane and sat, until a lady announced herself as Mme. Worms. This was too much for Horse & Hound & she fled (having read all W H Smith's fashion mags & no doubt snipped out any thing she fancied, shades of Lady Islington). The *dear* young man who had arranged the hat said "of course I wanted a fan as well &, you know, a bit of blue velvet, but the window isn't quite big enough."

Anyway I signed over 100 copies so they tell me & there were no embarrassing pauses. I *was* tired at the end.

. . . I'm reading Hester [Chapman]'s novel she sent me – very enjoyable.[31] Such a treat to read for pure pleasure again exactly what one feels inclined to. I shall take a year or two off & sharpen my wits a bit.

N.M.'s letter of 1 May, printed in Love from Nancy, *begins: "My crazy friend Prof. [Alan] Ross has written such a lovely pamphlet for la Société néo-philologique de Helsinki – on upper-class usage in English." She immediately recognised its potential for the Christmas market: "illustrated by Osbert Lancaster,[32] & entitled Are you U?" This opened the "U / non U" debate and led to N.M. editing and contributing to* Noblesse Oblige *the following year.*

---

31. *Falling Stream* by Hester Chapman (1899–1976). A novelist and biographer, married to Ronald Griffin, she had occasionally helped out in the bookshop.

32. Osbert Lancaster (1908–86), cartoonist and writer.

N.M.   6/5/54

. . . I'm *furious* about the book called ONE – the name I was reserving for my memoires. No no I'm not writing them, you needn't worry *yet*.

N.M.   14/6/54

I'm back [from Russia] – having had the most fascinating fortnight of my whole life. I think I must write it all down & send it to various buddies – no obligation to read. . . .[33]

While waiting to go into the Tomb I heard distinctly "brush" & the literal double of Derek Hill* trotted up with a wreath twice his own size – deposited it – bestowed glittering smiles on the pretty little Tartar guards & withdrew. It was a memorable moment & I longed for my brownie to snap it. Stalin the spit image of Vi Trefusis. Lenin looks at one out of the corner of his eye, very sinister indeed. They lie there like a dreadful old married couple . . .

N.M.   7/7/54

. . . I went to the Windsors for Sunday – they've got that old mill I once nearly took. All its charm has vanished & it has become a small little town – guests' rooms in all the cow sheds. A huge party of deadly Americans, all apparently *one's* age or a little less – all in fact between 80 & 90. The famous Mr. Donoghue[34] – behaving I must say, quite well & respectfully to both D & Dss. He is just like a Russian to look at, a face of pudge suet. . . .

---

33. N.M.'s "Diary of a Visit to Russia" was published in *The Water Beetle* eight years later.
34. See Christopher Wilson, *Dancing with the Devil: The Windsors and Jimmy Donahue* (2000).

N.M.   21/10/54

. . . I see Freya Stark's book is advertised as "a journey with Herodotus." Is that her pet name for Derek Hill? I'm trying to cook up an enormous new tease for him – so rare to find such a satisfactory victim.

1955

N.M.   6/2/55

This lovely paper is the price of shame. In return for 2 years' supply & £40 I'm allowing them to use my name in advertisements . . . Great junketings here for Teddy Boy [the Duke of Windsor], a dinner at the Embassy on Tuesday: everybody striving to be ELEGANT. I was especially keen on the lady who said all female writers are awful to look at – how cross Rosamond [Lehmann][35] would have been! . . . Heywood, I am being a bore – you must put £20 on my bill for expense of spirit – I mean it.

H.H.   22/2/55

Could the book on the Paris Embassy be "Gestapo, France, 1943–5"? I only thought it might be possible because didn't the Gestapo back on to the Embassy? . . . Anne & I went last night, with ghastly groans, to a thing called "a post-prandial punch party. Black tie. 9 till 11", at some people called Hanbury-Bateman, who live in Blomfield Road in the house next to yours. Hanbury-Bateman has become the local house bully. He is one of those terrifying live wires who means to clear everything up and clear everyone out. He insists on all houses being painted every four years and all form of rot, with which, of course, one is riddled, being hacked out at the cost of thousands. So far he has only been at work in Blomfield, which it is said he is turning into a millionaire's row. It'll be our turn next and we're sure to be flung into that workhouse for women in the Harrow Road. We went to post-

---

35. Rosamond Lehmann (1901–90), novelist.

prandial just in order to toady and stood for a hideous two hours being made to drink boiling gum and shriek at the new rich refined neighbours. Mrs Hanbury B seemed to be wearing a satinette bathing costume. Anne & I were both queer in the night . . .

N.M.   12/4/55

About Voltaire – what I'm after is a scholarly 19th Cent: edition of the letters, if such a thing exists (it must). These piecemeal early editions are never much good – the ones of Mme du Deffand I got from you are really useless, though nice pretty books which I'm fond of . . .

N.M.   16/4/55

. . . I guess I shall have to have the col: works of Voltaire, oh the torture because where to put him? Get a tidy copy if poss. . . . My article on the aristocracy [for *Encounter*]. I lovingly work away at it all day and think it the best thing I've ever done. It's a sort of anthology of teases – something for everybody. I think it will be safer to be in Greece when it appears.

N.M.   2/5/55

Here it is [a print?] – or will be. Such a typical scene when I went round just now.

Bookseller, proudly, "I've got it!"

N., gushing, "Oh you are wonderful."

B. "Alors! Où est-ce? Oh zut-alors – oh la-la – je l'ai mis où" He became scarlet with misery & fury – I said "Never mind, bring it round and I'll show you my pretty flat." Which is where we've got to – except that I've paid!

H.H.   5/5/55

. . . The Clique has been particularly hopeless and has failed to print my list for two weeks running so I can't give you any Voltaire news before I leave. I feel pretty gloomy about it because have been told by a serious dealer that that edition is far the best and costs over £100. Anyhow I shall tell Handy about it and, if there is an answer he must quote and report.

I am in a telescoped state trying to leave things trim [before going on holiday] and of course failing. A Surrealist book with an india-rubber breast on the cover[36] – left on approval by Pooter[37] many years ago – has just been unearthed by a Nanny in the children's room. A little Miss Chester-Beatty came in this afternoon and said "Is this Nancy Mitford's shop?" Things don't alter.

N.M.   25/5/55

. . . Would you do me a great kindness? In my article on Lords I've mentioned a list of houses which I assert are still inhabited. Doubt has been cast on one or two, & I do want to get it right, & now the page proofs have arrived & I imagine time is getting short [A list of great houses follows] . . . Could you also ask Malcolm [Bullock],[38] does he remember if the Adelphi belonged to some Lord? I'm nearly sure it did because I remember Robert [Byron][39] inveighing so tremendously against him.

---

36. Catalogue of the International Surrealist Exhibition, designed by Marcel Duchamp.
37. A nickname for Mr Merino, the book-runner, from George and Weedon Grossmith's *The Diary of a Nobody*.
38. Sir Malcolm Bullock (1890–1966), M.P., diplomat and francophile.
39. Robert Byron (1905–41), writer and traveller.

H.H.   13/9/55

Your letter came just as I was dashing off at dawn to catch a train back to the clique [the shop]. Anne drove me and we sat in crushed silence to the station where there was just time to pull the letter out and read it. It sent me into such fits that we were totally restored and I was still shrieking as I got into my carriage. You could make a splendid book from your abuse and should keep all letters but perhaps they will go into "I and Me make One" [mooted title of N.M.'s auto-biography] . . .

I may come bookbuying to Paris for a few nights during first week of Nov. and, if so, shall ask Geoffrey [Gilmour*] for a hammock . . .

On 22 September Encounter *wrote to N.M. saying that their September issue had had such a success that it was now out of print. They suggested reprinting her article, "The English Aristocracy", separately and presenting it to any enquirers.*

At the foot of the letter N.M. wrote: "Don't want to be difficult with them, but my gorge rises at the idea of giving anything away. What about Anne's copy which I hear is annotated by furious aristos, illustrated by O. Lancaster, with extracts from some of the letters I've received? Hot cakes, I should have said, for Christmas?"

H.H.   26/9/55

I am also outraged at the thought of a thousand free articles . . . I am still a wreck after Brian Howard's flying visit last week. He had given Mrs H[oward] and fishcake⁴⁰ the slip to come and "arrange" about the sale of his father's pictures at

---

40. Brian Howard's boyfriend since 1943. Usually called Sam, he was, in fact, Denis Langford.

Christie's. He rang us up at home when he arrived at 8 and said he was coming round. He arrived at 11 and stayed till 3. He had taken a room at the Ritz but begged us to let him sleep in the armchair and was incensed when we would not. He fell to the floor and, stuffing a ten thousand franc note between Anne's legs said "I am going to give you an Iron Crown, Ducky. The Iron Crown of the Queens of Hungary." Taxis came and went furiously away. The next day he borrowed £50 from the shop and the next day he wanted 30 more, so I gave it him myself and he gave me cheques on Swiss banks and today there's a telegram from Mrs H saying stop cheques. The last night he asked us to have a drink at the Ritz (did you know there are bibles by everyone's beds?) . . . Dinner at Bentley's and, when we were turned out of there, there were ten fearful minutes left to catch the aeroplane. He mimicked the refined voices of the air hostesses and the whole terminal was in tumult with loudspeakers shrieking for him. Very drunk myself, I became Napoleonic and pushed him past fainting hostesses and into the bus . . .

N.M.   1/2/56

... My Dutch translator has written to say shall he call
Hun's (sic)[41] cupboard "the cave of the nobles"? ...

N.M.   28/2/56

I long for you [to come to Paris]. I'm entertaining some 40
literateurs on Friday [March] 16 to meet you – a rival party to
the Embassy one for Q Mother.

Mrs Ham[mersley] says she got two letters on the same day
from the Riviera. Me: "The snow looks so pretty & there are
masses of amusing people here, I'm having a lovely time."
The Other: "All is ruin & desolation, tourists sleeping in
unheated schools as the hotels can't have them etc." ...

PS Here's a list so that you'll know more or less who they
all are. I've put "to meet Mr HH" on the cards. I rather long
for it, far more than parties for les gens du monde because
they enjoy it more. [List followed overleaf]

N.M.   undated   (postcard)

Enid Macleod of the British Council says her telephone has
been hot all day with puzzled intellectuals, eager to be in the
swim, saying who is M. Aywood Eel? ... I'm sure they think
you're a kind of Samuel Beckett.

N.M.   3/4/56

... Do you know anybody who could easily & told for chil-

---

41. The Hons, from *The Pursuit of Love*.

dren tell me the difference between Newton & Descartes? Perhaps in 2 or 3 sentences . . .

I wrote & told Mrs Ham to order Legacy[42] on my acc-[ount] which I've no doubt she has keenly done. I did the same to my good Mama who replied that she is abonnée to Harrods. How different people are . . .

N.M.   12/4/56

I've been wriggling like an eel over Voltaire, writing to see if L[ondon] L[ibrary] can lend it to me. But they would rather not put it in the post, which I do understand. It looks too lovely – I guess I'd better have it. In the end I shall have quite an impressive collection of 18th century stuff . . .

Now for the U Book [*Noblesse Oblige*]. An absolutely blissful person flew over to interview me about it called [Anne] Scott James.[43] Sunday Express. Terribly beautiful & elegant. Evelyn says those nice ones are always the worst . . .

N.M.   14/4/56

On reflection & taking into account the fact that I never could afford the whole edition, also that I go up to 1750 in my book so there are still 10 years left blank, I think I won't buy any [Voltaire]. I'm so sorry to have caused such trouble . . .

N.M.   29/4/56

. . . *Voltaire*. I'm going to be an unpardonable bore & just get the requisite letters from the L.L. £90 is too much – I could have run to £40. Don't care about the binding as anyway there's no room on my shelves for it. Do be nice & understand, I know you will.

---

42. Novel by Sybille Bedford (b. 1911).
43. Anne Scott James (b. 1913), journalist and writer.

H.H.   24/5/56   Chinon
(postcard of a 1920ish simpering "beauty")

Here's an early snap of Violet [Trefusis]. Have had a heavenly [French] tour in spite of Anne having had German measles. Furiously back to school on Monday.

N.M.   18/6/56   Torcello, Venice

Now. One of the waiters here, aged 11, very clever, hopes to be a doctor (fat & sweet) hopes soon to learn English. Picture book for him. Another aged 16, now reading Wells's History of the World, knows a *little* English – something easy with pictures. And two more waiters about 18. If Britain in Pictures were still going, something like that for them.

Then a naughty boy of about 5 who loves money & whom I tease & torture. Have you any ideas? He sells awful little gilded sea horses. No hurry & I'll send you the names, they'll like to have parcels, I guess.

N.M.   29/6/56   Torcello, Venice

. . . The books: perfection. As I know you've forgotten what you said, please send: 1030 Words; Pictures of Br.; Picture Book of Britain; Giant Golden Encycl. to Signor Georgio Rossi at this address, but after I've gone as giving makes me shy. He can do it for me.

N.M.   7/7/56   Torcello, Venice

. . . I've come to a sort of ½ way house with my book, so I read it all through yesterday. It's better than I thought. Uphill work, though, compared with Pomp.

N.M.   14/7/56   Hyères

You won't forget the 4 books for Giorgio Rossi . . . We all cried when I left. It *is* a heavenly place. G Rossi said, "Now you go, to whom can I ask about modern intellectuals?" The gens du monde in Venice all think I'm a dangerous Communist & that it's rather dashing to know me at all (I do wish Mr Paul Johnson[44] could be told) . . .

H.H.   19/7/56

I ought to have written before to tell you that I did send all the boys' and girls' books off to Torcello. The same day you ordered them. They say now that book post to Italy takes an eternity . . . I asked Osbert Lancaster for tit bits about Evelyn's dance – but he said that none of his hopes were fulfilled. E himself, he said, was in disappointingly mellow form. Osbert asked the daughter where her dear father was. "Upstairs with the good champagne" she answered. What Osbert and Evelyn did not seem to know or to have noticed & what Jonny Gathorne-Hardy* told me was that, at one moment in the early morning, an army of real tarts arrived and started climbing over the garden railings. A strange and unprofitable venture, one would imagine. Jonny himself was solicited by one of them . . .

Malcolm [Bullock] goes to grander balls. The one at Syon never came to life & Loelia Westminster's[45] comment was dead right – "I felt as if I had spent four hours in a morgue." Such a contrast, he went on, to the Norfolks' dance at St James's Palace where the old had stuck on their last aigrettes & were enjoying themselves like anything . . .

---

44. Paul Johnson (b. 1928), historian, editor and journalist.
45. Loelia Duchess of Westminster (1902–93), wife of the 2nd Duke of Westminster (1930–47) and author of *Grace and Favour*.

When we got back from last weekend, we found our back door smashed & Trelawny's[46] pistol and Lucy's* purse gone and the bust of the Empress Eugenie smashed in the garden. Handy says exactly the same happened in Sherlock Holmes.

N.M.   8/8/56   Hyères

No, I'm not got down by V[oltaire], only by the cuttings which have got out of control since every sort of local trade paper speaks of U and me on any & every pretext! . . . A friend sent Noblesse cuttings from USA & all FOR except one which raked up me turning down 5000 dollars a week & said that must be regarded as a Communist activity!

N.M.   18/8/56

. . . A huge cutting from a Dutch paper describes me as N.M. Schrijfster, femme du monde, enfant terrible. Gracious, what is schrijfster one asks oneself. The Dutchman who sends it writes to me describing a visit to London "I liked best an afternoon in some Club where Stephen Spender & 25 other poets recited their poetry". "I visited the Daily Telegraph – everywhere wonderful hospitality." "I have written the first 80 chapters of my new novel Jeunesse Dorée" . . .

Oh dear, such a lot to do after all these weeks – 3 months. Don't know where to start. *Thirty* parcels of books including a huge one from you I haven't the courage to open!

N.M.   3/9/56

. . . You are to have the treat of an omnibus Mitford – keenly sabotaged, no *doubt* by Handysides . . .

---

46. Edward Trelawny, alleged friend of Byron and author of *Adventures of a Younger Son* (1831). He was a relation of Anne Hill.

N.M. *was having considerable difficulty with her eyes and several letters refer to recommendations for oculists. "I rather dread doctors at one's age, it always seems to me they take one look at you, cry cancer & remove several important portions of your anatomy."*

N.M.   7/9/56

. . . I would like a book plate, simply Nancy Mitford like the Baskerville Bible title page, lots of squiggles. Could you ponder? . . .

N.M.   22/9/56

The bottom one, perfect & perfect size, so go ahead with it . . . Mollie [Buchanan] sent a bill which is one of the most brilliant works of fiction I ever read . . . Many of the books I'm supposed to have bought I've never even heard of. "People" 2 gns. What sort of people. It sounds lovely. Oh the *bliss* of the shop . . .

N.M.   7/10/56

Fiction *was* a joke, but it would be a help, when a bill is over 3 years old, if M would put who the books were sent to . . .

Besterman[47] came to see me. He is plainly not delighted that I am treading on his ground – his opening words: Why do you waste your time writing about Voltaire? He intends to write the definitive life when he has finished the letters . . .

Lovely visit from Widow.[48] We lunched at Embassy & she said to Cynthia [Jebb*] did the P.M. [Anthony Eden] seem

---

47. Theodore Besterman (1904–76), the leading Voltaire scholar, whose collection now forms the core of the Taylorian Institution Library at Oxford University.
48. Mrs Violet Hammersley.

very *low* when he was here? Not at all, on top of the world. Gloomy silence, then, "And when you were alone with Clarissa,[49] did she not *break down*?"

N.M. 19/10/56

Oh isn't it lovely [the bookplate]? . . . Can we start with 500 or do I have to stoke up for life? Goodness what a sticking and licking there'll be – yes please, gum . . .

N.M. 3/11/56

I hear that Handy has banned the bus (Mitford Omni). Can't blame him, who would buy it when they can have the great works in Penguin – not me.

I'm to be televised in my lovely home . . . Felt I couldn't deprive everybody of such a wicked gloat . . .

N.M. 17/11/56

You'll never Clique anything for me again but oh 20 volumes [of Carlyle]. What would Marie [her maid] say & where could I put them? . . . What I want is Fred:, Fr. rev: & Cromwell. You know my flat & now there's not room for another bookcase. Every month I give at least 20 books to "the students" who come for them with a sack – many French writers now send me their books, with fulsome dedicaces all of which go into the sack! Unread of course . . .

H.H. 9/11/56

. . . Don't get too much advance cold feet about coming [to London]. The only voluptuous thing that THEY have done so far is to ask ONE not to motor for pleasure. You will be

---

49. Lady Eden (b. 1920), later Countess of Avon.

motoring for purpose. They won't start switching off fires till at least Jan. and then it's more likely to just be oil fires (Snape is entirely heated by oil). The only people I have heard squabbling about Suez are Brian [Howard] and John Banting.[50] "You are just a stupid semi-Communist, my dear, I don't mind how many people get killed. I only care about Places – places like the Pitti" ...

Brian's party was surprisingly mild ... I fear that Brian may be too ill now to be more than mild but perhaps I shall know better after he has come to dinner tomorrow.

Harold [Acton]'s party didn't begin till ten. Anne & I, after dinner, struggled unwillingly into evening dresses and set off in cold blood. All I could see at first was Anne Rosse[51] spread on a sofa and covered in possible camellias. Anne (my one) gave a little wail and settled behind another sofa and started to look at Harold's book. – There were supper tables and a vast spread. Perhaps it was me being shopworn but I didn't feel that it "went" – in spite of the fizzing of Paddy L[eigh] F[ermor].[52]

N.M.   27/11/56

... Could you send Legacy to La Baronne de Gail ... She knitted me bedsocks on hearing I was going to England, & another friend arrived today with a lovely pink shawl. I feel like a Hungarian refugee ...

50. John Banting (1902–72), artist.
51. Countess of Rosse (1902–92), mother of Lord Snowdon.
52. Patrick Leigh Fermor (b. 1915), traveller and writer.

1957

N.M.   26/1/57

... I think M Palewski 1 rue Bonaparte Paris VI had better
have The Nude.[53]

N.M.   21/2/57

The Vision [TV profile "in my lovely home"]. Such a
fuming press, absolutely no similarity so that you didn't feel
they could be writing about the same thing. Pure delight says
one, a drearier half hour I never spent, says another. Mostly
rather anti, & quite a few said I was too busy playing
at ladies. I was really far too terrified to play at anything –
TERRIFIED ...

H.H.   26/3/57

Mrs Hammersley has just been in with just a gold shell
hatpin gleaming from under the layers of veils. She was here,
she said because of her 80th birthday and could she borrow a
book so of course I gave her one ...

Do you know what a fearful thing you landed me in? When
I came back from my jury, Handy told me about that letter he
had written you about R[andolph] Churchill[54] and the Pentagon. It made me tremble because I at once foresaw all that
came to pass. R Churchill came in with Ld. Stanley[55] and by

---

53. Kenneth Clark's *The Nude*, 1957; for Gaston Palewski, see note 15.
54. Randolph Churchill (1911–68), journalist and only son of Winston
Churchill.
55. Lord Stanley of Alderley (1907–71), "Ed", a cousin of N.M., often
mentioned in contemporary memoirs.

bad luck I was alone in the front shop and they bore down upon me with beating-up looks on their faces. "Why am I no more welcome here than a Russian in the Pentagon? All I have ever done is not to pay my bill." And then a lot of facetious things about country bumpkins which I didn't undertand (Secretly I didn't even know what the Pentagon is). In the middle of it all Handy came in & scuttled to the basement like a dodgy rabbit though, when I accused him of rank cowardice afterwards, he declared that he did not know what was going on. Umbrage was very nearly reached. What's so dreadful is that I know you are only shrieking . . .

N.M.   27/3/57

V[ictor] C[unard]56 was here when your letter arrived, so I began reading it out to him but shrieked so much I couldn't go on. Oh *dear*, are you unscathed? I say, Handy isn't much of a hero – what will happen when gunmen come for the bill? . . .

My quiet American has typed about 20,000 words of my book. He says it is so fascinating it doesn't seem like work – oh I do hope others will find the same . . .

N.M.   Easter Monday 1957

. . . I've just had a *vivid* dream of the shop. Handy was trying to make me buy a book called Plastic Cookery in the shape of a shining pink frying pan. He kept saying in threatening tones the dishes are all very expensive. I was glad when Marie appeared with my breakfast!

---

56. Victor Cunard (1898– 1960), diplomat who settled in Venice. Sadly, N.M.'s letters to him were destroyed by his brother.

On the way to stay in Ireland with the Devonshires at
Lismore, N.M. had a day or two in London where she dined
with H.H. and Anne: "awfully nice gossip we had didn't we!"*

N.M.   18/7/57   Bauer-Grunewald, Venice

. . . I went to Torcello: all pleased to see me & the holy
sacristan had read The Blessing in Italian, & said he now
perfectly understands the English mentality, hitherto so
mysterious!

H.H.   6/8/57

I have sent you Ste B[euve] and B[ourbon]s of Naples. You
might get a seedy shriek out of Lucky Jim[57] but I somehow
doubt if Mrs [Iris] Murdoch would be your thing.

I have read a proof of V[oltaire] in L[ove] & was of course
fascinated. I think you have done it brilliantly – it so scintil-
lates. Just think of the toppling heaps that we shall be able to
have here to thunder down on costumiers. I especially liked
Mme. du C[hâtelet]'s rules for behaving – though of course
one never acts them. The wonder and fascination of the way
they all went on. Anne was also enthralled.

N.M.   7/8/57

That Italian – can't remember his name – has sent me a
cheque for 10,000 francs for his bill. Fearfully mean of him as
the 1000 franc note isn't worth £1 & of course that's why he
has done it . . . I've a good mind not to cash it & make him
send the proper amount after the official devaluation . . .

Is it true you send books to [Guy] Burgess[58] to be trans-

---

57. Kingsley Amis's best-known novel, published in 1954.
58. Guy Burgess (1911– 63), diplomat and spy.

lated? If so, it's your plain duty to send Voltaire, the Father of the French Revolution.

H.H.   9/8/57

So sorry about Albertini. He's what Handy calls "one of my crosses" and now he's become one of yours . . . How I long for the arrival of you and Pooter. I'm sure we'd do terrific biz what with you signing and Pooter pooting . . .

Pam Berry[59] came in to bully yesterday and said we must fill the window with the English Review (Altrincham) [critical of H.M. The Queen]. Handy stood to his refusing gun though was sweating by the end. I don't quite know what the shop line is. Torn between bolsh and tweed I suppose age tends to tweed. But can one cure stupidity?

N.M.   12/8/57

. . . Really Pam Berry. I am shocked. Gaston thinks there is a plot against the Queen & he says nothing could be more wickedly stupid. What do such as Pam want? What can the answer be but mischief?

N.M.   15/9/57

. . . There was a very funny fuss about Cecil [Beaton]'s cover. He was here, & I got a hysterical letter from Jamie saying this cover will utterly stop anybody buying the book, & YOU must tell Cecil it won't do. Meanwhile I was thinking this is far the best cover of my books. Of course I won the day – glad to see that you agree with me.

---

59. Lady Pamela Berry (1914–82), later Lady Hartwell, distinguished political hostess.

Now that the book is being printed, I've found two ghastly mistakes on which the critics are sure to feast. Ay di me! . . .

Jacques Brousse came yesterday & said he loves Italy because the people are so poor & unemployed that they have to be agreeable. As my heart had been *wrung* in Venice by this very fact so that I felt it did away with much of one's pleasure, I nearly hit him . . .

1958

You may have seen in today's TIMES that Brian Howard
has died. It's a sad story. He rang me up from Nice on Sunday
morning a week ago to say that Sam had been found dead on
the bathroom floor of their newly built villa. He said that the
workmen had not fitted the escape pipe of the geyser properly
and that it was a non-smelling gas and so Sam was suffocated.
Brian wanted me to get hold of John Banting and give him
money to fly out as soon as possible. I spent the whole day
finding Banting. He lives in a lodging at Chiswick which
is not on the telephone. One is supposed to ring up a pub
who will take a message but the pub never answers. I sent a
telegram and eventually a peasant rang me up to say that
Banting was away staying with Roger Senhouse[60] in Rye
but he did not know the address. I rang up several hundred
people – most of them away but those who weren't only knew
that the house was somewhere in Rye High Street. One is
allowed to send a telegram to Chiswick on a Sunday but not
to Rye. The police will deliver telegrams in cases of an emer-
gency but only before a person is dead not afterwards. I never
knew those rules before. He [Banting] got the telegram on
Monday afternoon and I gave him the money and he flew to
Nice on Tuesday. This last Monday I had a letter from him to
say that the night of the day after he got there, Brian took too
many sleeping pills and died. He said that Brian had not
meant to kill himself and that he had only taken a few too

---

60. Roger Senhouse (1899–1970), publisher, translator and friend of
Lytton Strachey.

many. I believe him but nobody else will. I remember once when Brian spent the night at Warwick Av. on the sofa, he took too many by mistake. The person who the whole thing is really ghastly for is Brian's mother who was there when all this happened. I suppose too that there will be awful money complications what with death duties and bills for villas and yachts pouring in. I wish it had been Eddie [Gathorne-Hardy] instead of Banting who had gone out as Eddie would have been much more calm and practical and useful to Mrs H . . .

A man has just been in to ask if we will tear 3 illustrations out of a new art book in the window for him.

N.M.   23/1/58

Oh! No, I didn't see it. I feel most dreadful sad & have the usual guilt feelings inseparable from these occasions. One must be nicer to one's friends. You really did come up trumps & you must be so glad now that you took all those desperate measures to get hold of Banting . . . I suppose if Sam had to die, poor old Brian would rather go too in a way. Goodness. I *mind* . . .

I'll write to Mrs H, I've got the address. It's quite appalling for her, isn't it? I often think people miss wicked old creatures like Brian far more than normal, satisfactory, city-going, church-going ones. I suppose it will be more peaceful without him, but he really seemed to have turned over a new leaf.

N.M.   18/2/58

. . . How awful of Brian not to have made a will. I suppose he'd have said on his death bed, Don't let poor Sammie starve.

I'm working on a film, possibly for Alec Guinness. It amuses me very much. But oh! the awfulness of the film world & how glad I am I can earn my living without it.

N.M.   25/2/58

. . . No, one book about Gov: slang will do. It's for a film
scenario I'm toiling over – I want the French crooks to talk
American tough, so the book you've sent must be perfect . . .
Spender has asked me to write an article called My Utopia.
Well, my Utopia consists of cottagers, happy in their cottages
while I am being happy in the Big House. So I'm afraid it
would make everybody furious with me.

In April Hamish Hamilton submitted Voltaire in Love *to the
Readers' Union in the hope that it might print a huge edition
for its members. Their director wrote back: "I am afraid*
Voltaire in Love *won't do. The book calls, I think, for a
degree of sophistication, even cynicism about sex, which
I am afraid does not exist, and which would be considered
undesirable in any case, by our members. I hope you will
understand."* N.M. *photocopied this and in her accompanying
letter wrote, "Is this not delightful? Throw away when read."*

N.M.   21/8/58   Inch Kenneth, Isle of Mull

. . . Beautiful here, but dull. My mother, who says she lives
here because there are no tourists, simply scans the mainland
with her telescope & as soon as a tent appears she sends the
boat & the occupants are brought over & given an enormous
tea. Two perfectly amazed women in trousers were yesterday's catch. "Sort of Miss Husseys", my mother said in a loud
aside (Miss Hussey was an old gov of ours).

N.M.   2/10/58   Château de Fontaines les Nonnes

. . . Exchange with Cecil B:
N. Handy tells me far the best book of the autumn is a life
of Kitchener.

Cecil. Oh *dear*. Who wrote it?

N. The man who wrote that smashing life of Mr Gladstone [Philip Magnus[61]].

---

61. Sir Philip Magnus-Allcroft (1906–88), historian and biographer.

1959

N.M. 8/1/59   Château de Fontaines les Nonnes

. . . I missed Handasyde's piece in the Teleg[raph] this year –
I've been busy doing O & sometimes forget the papers. If you
could get a cutting, I promise to return it – always so amusing
to see what sells. I see in an advert that Grim-Grin [Graham
Greene] comes first . . .

N.M. 20/1/59

. . . Will you please have P[ursuit] of L[ove] bound in citron
morocco & moled [N.M.'s cipher was a mole] & sent to an
address I'll give you when ready. It's for a fan who is considerably helping me to formulate a new novel & this seems a suitable reward . . .

H.H. 27/2/59

I hope something terrible hasn't happened. Mr Hobson has
put moles on that bound P. of Love. I can't remember if you
told me to mole it. Otherwise Mr Hobson did it off his own
bat, as Handy might say. Anyhow the book does look stunning.
I hope that you won't be appalled by the price which is £8. I
promise I haven't put on more than the weeniest per cent . . .

N.M. 8/3/59

. . . Can you wait for Casement?[62] I'll send, with *pleasure*,
wrapped in Coward, but it must be at your risk. Can't help
feeling they'd be sure to spot . . .

---

62. *Roger Casement: The Black Diaries*, published by Grove Press in 1959,
was banned in England.

H.H.   9/3/59

So sorry to give you such Casement trouble and I didn't know that it was gross in size as well as indecency. If Diana [Mosley] or Noel Coward cannot smuggle, I will myself when I probably pass through in May to join Anne and her mother in S. of France . . . Old Driberg[63] can jolly well wait for his vomit . . .

Mollie showed me your letter to her. First I'd heard about us smashing up here.[64] I think it's only winter fungus . . .

There was a young man in the shop this morning in old suede shoes, khaki trousers, blue mack – the pincher school of clothes in fact & he spent hours of shelf snooping. Handy wrote me a palsied scribble on his pad WHO IS THIS MAN? He said he would buy four books & asked Handy to tot. Handy did but showed him the pad with WHO IS THIS MAN? on it. Pincher said he would come back with the £17 in cash but never has – so we're wondering.

N.M.   17/3/59

. . . Debo is here & I'd squared her to take Casement & then somebody gave her Lolita[65] so I can't let her take a whole library of dirty books as well as several Dior dresses, Can I? What a bore . . .

Sir Allen Lane[66] came to luncheon here, he is awfully agreeable & praised your shop to the skies. I didn't tell him that Anne used to complain that people wore out the carpet & then bought a Penguin (6d) . . . There's a Penguin exhibition

---

63. Tom Driberg (1905–76), journalist with "a threefold passion: Socialism, Sex and God."
64. The first allusion to the row between the Hills and the Buchanans.
65. Novel by Vladimir Nabokov (1899–1977), published in 1959 and initially banned in Britain.
66. Sir Allen Lane (1902–70), publisher and founder of Penguin Books.

here with a life-sized photograph of ME, do be impressed. I went to the opening & was quite embarrassed.

N.M.   25/5/59

... The head people of Stock [French publishers] got MGM to run The Blessing[67] for them (so that they could decide how big a reprinting to make of it in French) – never asked me! Somebody told them I was very cross, at a lunch, & the excuse was that I might have demonstrated as it's quite different from the book. A. who was there said: "you don't know Nancy, nothing would shake her sang-froid."

N.M.   10/9/59

Shrieking over an invitation to "close the annual session of American Women's Activities with a speech on World Citizenship". "They (the audience) are efficient women & present a lovely sight of feminine charm as well. The atmosphere is one of eagerness, positive thinking & fun." The meeting takes place at Berchtesgarden, shades of Bobo!![68] *Naturally* I have accepted ...

N.M.   16/9/59

The clockwork mouse [lawyer] says – has been saying for ages – that the shop is not a good investment for somebody who lives abroad. Very possibly true. But I have explained that I can't sell my share to some rapacious stranger. There's no hurry whatever, but if some solution to the problem could be arrived at, it might be best for all concerned. Positive thinking is necessary here – cheerfulness & fun are not likely to be absent ... Mouse thought you all *lovely*.

---

67. See note 3.
68. Bobo was Unity Mitford.

With N.M. writing Don't Tell Alfred, *she needed help over modern youth. In a letter of 16/10/59 she asked for the sort of psychoanalyst's jargon useful in the context of Fanny's bearded son – "also a little Zen jargon – don't kill yourself, only if it's easy." Later she thought she would have "to visit Blighty in search of a bit of copy."*

N.M.   2/10/59

. . . Ask Jonny Gathorne-Hardy for one or two crimes (not sex) & would they lead to the [therapist's] couch or the sack? I've got to get 2 naughty boys away from Eton. They can run away but I prefer a good sacking with bell, book & candle – perhaps that doesn't occur nowadays?

H.H.   23/10/59

Zen jargon ought to be easy. I think that a book called The Spirit of Zen[69] might be the ticket. Oddly, the psycho-analysing seems more difficult . . . Christmas tentacles begin to wave. Not that I mean don't ask any more Zen qs. Do, I like to try.

N.M.   28/10/59

. . . No hurry about psychoanalysis, as it can go in later. I think I can manage Zen – oh well, send The Spirit, might have some jokes. I read the bit about Diana Coo[per] to her and she passed it & was even quite cross that she doesn't reappear in the book . . .

---

69. A. Watts, *The Spirit of Zen* (new impression, 1959).

1960

. . . I was alone in the shop at the end of last Saturday morning and in a hurry to go out to lunch at ¼ to 1. As I locked the shop door into the hall, I was aware of a woman coming in at the front door but saw her rattling the flat doors and thought she was going up above, so I slammed the front door. On Monday morning I discovered that it had been Lady Theo Cadogan[70] – a customer even dottier than most. She failed to open the front door again & thought she was imprisoned in that small space. She poked her umbrella through the letterbox and banged it to and fro – screaming all the time – but no one heard. Then, with her umbrella, she smashed the glass fanlight over the front door. A passing American was disturbed by the crashing glass & called two policemen. They rang the flat bells so that all the tenants came pouring down. They thought the shop was being burgled & carried the pictures in the hall to their flats. The charwoman said that the policemen cut their hands on the glass and that there were pools of blood, but that was the only exaggeration. Luckily I was out when Ly Theo called on Monday, so Handy gave her a soothing talk. She seemed none the madder.

This was the only occasion of a customer being caught in the hall between the front door of the shop and the outside door to the street. It is more difficult to imagine nowadays since the front door was moved, by the landlord, several feet nearer

---

70. Lady Theo Cadogan (d. 1977), daughter of the 4th Earl of Gosford, widow of Sir Alec Cadogan, diplomat.

*the outside door in 1985. Lady Theo's imprisonment
remained a famous episode, recounted to all who came
to work in the shop.*

For the rest of 1960 no other H.H. letters survive.

N.M.   Venice 21/7/60

. . . Harold A[cton] has been here. In his hotel is a Mrs
Moats, rich old yankee bore, hideous (ex-beauty) & lonely.
He & the Sutros [John & Gillian][71] spent their time escaping
from her & really enjoying the chase. Then she rang him
up & said "you son of a bitch, you stayed with me for a week
in Mexico City & you haven't asked me to a cup of tea."
"Misses *Moats*, considering the rumours you *spread* about
my MOEURS . . ." It went on for an hour – wouldn't one give
one's life for a recording? . . .

John has written a series of obscene poems of things supposed to have been overheard by Mrs Moats while crossing
the Rialto. So dreadful even I am not allowed to see them.

N.M.   17/8/60

. . . A young journalist came to see me yesterday & said, if
you have 3 wishes, what would they be & I said I really can't
think except of course I would like to be rich & I then saw
that *he* thought I was rich & was amazed by such cupidity.

*In September there is a letter from Handasyde Buchanan
which Nancy, for once, kept and from which I have selected
some excerpts.*

Handasyde Buchanan   6/9/60

I have read THE GREAT WORK [*Don't Tell Alfred*] and of

---

71. John Sutro (1904–85), film producer and inimitable mimic.

course I enjoyed it enormously, and I do think that you have, over all, brought it off again. The characters big and small are splendid – I love Mockbar and better still Bouche-B. I think I enjoyed Harold Nicolson's visit best (it is *perfect*), then all the bits about the children, and Lady Leone's trespassing least, but I read that just after dinner when very tired and perhaps a little drunk so I may well be wrong. I feel I could really read it all over again which must be a good sign . . . [He followed this with some questions & pointed out some spelling mistakes.] We shall sell it like anything; I have arranged for a splendid new poster to arrive in two days. Now that I have finished it, I think I have enjoyed it more than LCC or Blessing, less than P of L . . .

N.M. [to H.H.] 2/10/60

I'm so delighted that you like it – that's very good news. Gov: publisher, Mr Cass Canfield, who always seems quite a human being (for a gov:) says, I congratulate you on a distinguished novel. Not a word about it being, possibly, drole. If I know the critics, they won't crack a smile, they never do. What I foresee & slightly dread is Ole Nole [Noël Coward], whose novel comes out the same day, dedicated to me, & I will be reviewed together as two old has-beens. Never mind, the public is faithful . . .

What *are* we to do about the [clockwork] mouse? Having wound it up, I now long for it to run down again. I'm coming over for the book, so then we must see what's what. Its last exploit was to write & tell me Prod[72] was drowned in a flood. When I got a letter saying as you were, I told Mrs Ham "He's quite all right – at last some good news;" she said "you don't think he may be half drowned?" She was wonderful about

---

72. Hon. Peter Rodd (1904–68), N.M.'s husband from 1933 to 1957.

Ostorog [her Turkish friend who had died suddenly] (who was bright & brilliant all day). "I could see he was gravely eel." "How could you?" "He made a little noise before speaking." "I say, that's funny – so do *you*."

N.M.   26/11/60

. . . A Dutchman has just sent the translation of his review of Alfred . . . "the author is blessed with an anormously big talent – this is mature art in extremely soigné style . . ."

About the shares. Now that you have the Royal Arms, I will take £4000 for them – it is my last word.

N.M.   5/12/60

. . . Réalités came to interview me. "Are you on top of the bestsellers?" "How little you know my compatriots. At the head of the bestsellers there is always an animal – Elsa the lioness has now been elbowed out by an otter."[73]

Jacques Brousse is hysterically translating Alf – he rings up every hour to ask what things mean.

N.M.   31/12/60

Is it my bullying [over her shares] which finally knocked you over? Then again, what does Handasyde mean by "audible grumbling"? . . . You must get *Réalités* Feb. no. in which I speak much more ungrudgingly than HB of Alf about the bookshop – *I* might have mentioned audible grumbles in *that* context. "Petit, mais situé en Mayfair et de tout premier ordre" is what in fact I say.

---

73. The references are to Joy Adamson's *Born Free* and Gavin Maxwell's *Ring of Bright Water.*

1961

N.M.　(postcard undated)

For your eye alone, Evelyn says, "Handy has all the concealed malice of the underdog. . . . Be sure & give me H's telephone number [Harriet Hill* was due to visit Paris] or, better
still, could she telephone to me here when she arrives? It's
difficult to get on to these girls as they are always out (how
sinister) . . .

N.M.　13/1/61

The naughty thing has never made a sign & I can't get on to
her as either the number is engaged (telephoning no doubt to
sly-faced youths in high black boots) or she is out (with said
youths in hot pursuit I expect). The boring thing is I'm going
away for 10 days – do wish I could have seen her . . .

N.M.　28/1/61

Harriet came & kept me in fits of laughter. I must say it's
too amusing seeing the children & having no responsibility
attached. "Lucy [Hill,* her sister] (aged 12?) is longing to
meet Tara (aged 13?) again & have an affair with him – & I
must say I wouldn't mind it myself." . . . I'm sure Harriet's all
right & she's simply loving it. I didn't think her coat was
warm enough (it can be very cold in Feb) & said, make your
father send you £5 to buy a rabbit lining at the Printemps. She
said it wouldn't be any good because she would never get
beyond the scent & the scarves if she had £5 in her pocket – I
thought this awfully endearing. I asked if she would care to
come to Lanvin & was surprised that she seemed to like the
idea – I always thought the black stocking brigade despised

our sort of clothes? But perhaps she thinks it will be a good laugh . . . There's a question of my doing the text of an illustrated book on Versailles? But does anybody read these books? . . .

H.H.   31/1/61

Angelic of you to have asked Harriet. Thank you so very much. I had a letter from her yesterday. This is what she says: "I went to lunch with Nancy yesterday, all alone with her, very nice and she laughed which pleased me – she's going to take me to the Lanvin collection, rather a thrill." I believe she could be weaned from black stockings – she has a genuine feel for clothes –, so it would be splendid for her to see a collection . . . I am sending her a fiver for the rabbit skin & telling her she must put on honourable blinkers past the scent and scarves . . . I think that the people who buy those big photo books DO read the text (think of Mary McCarthy's one on Venice[74]). They would certainly read it if it was by you.

N.M.   3/2/61

So we went to Lanvin but oh dear the clothes are so depressing. A great bore as I need a dinner dress & where to find one? I think Harriet enjoyed it but I got too tired & had to leave her sitting there. Overheard by Bettina B: "Who is that beatnik with Nancy?" "Probably a Duke's daughter or else the leading Englishwoman of letters." Do you like it? She isn't really beatnik, only perhaps the hair – she had a very nice get-up indeed. Promises that she will faithfully buy a rabbit . . . Seems sad to miss the spring here, having endured the winter. She's most companionable, isn't she? – so chatty & yet no nonsense.

---

74. Mary McCarthy, *Venice Observed*, 1956; first published in England in 1961.

H.H.   17/2/61

Thanks so much for Réalités which I'd been longing for. I was delighted by your benevolent description of this tiny first-class kennel for underdogs. THE underdog rather whistled at your saying that the hours are from 9 till 6 but I dared to point out that, from my own worm's-eye-view, I seemed to see that it was he who shortened them to pub-opening time. . . .

[Harriet] wrote saying that there was a coat she MUST have for £270 but pathetically adding that she would be content with a fiver for the under-rabbit. She continues to write ecstatic letters . . . Anne & I will discover more when we come . . .

The till was taken with £60 in it one evening last week by two Teds who scooped it from the dummy box under Handy's & my noses – though we didn't discover till the next morning . . .

H.H. proposed coming between 6 and 13 March but N.M. had arranged a jaunt in Italy "with Debo", starting on 6 March. "Couldn't you possibly come on the 4th? I can hardly bear it if I don't see you – & then my flat is looking so pretty with the new pictures etc."

N.M.   20/2/61

. . . Harriet has faded from my life – my own fault. The trouble is the impossibility of getting her on the telephone . . . I was pleased with Réalités. One looks a human being & they didn't invent a single word I hadn't said – so rare. English papers might well copy this system . . .

What clever Teds – or was it an INSIDE JOB?

N.M. put off her departure from Paris for a couple of days and suggested that they all meet up, together with Geoffrey

Gilmour, in a local restaurant: "best food for the price (about £2 each) in Paris."

N.M.   8/4/61   Fontaines

. . . Three American papers, NY Times, Sat Review & Newsweek have given Alf "rave" notices. NYT says her best novel. *Isn't it too queer?* Won't sell it however, Yanks don't buy books.

H.H.   25/4/61

Sorry not to have written. My father died last week, so I was away for some days & up to the neck in hideous arrangements & tangles especially as Sheila* [his sister] is abroad & can't help. People keep writing to tell me that it was a MER-CIFUL RELEASE & so I suppose in a way it was, but he was a kind nice father & very tolerant about one not going to hounds & making runs, which he would have really liked one to do – so I shall miss him. . . .

Handy has gone away for two days to write a book about cricket[75] (he really does seem able to write a book in two days), so the Bootle-Wilbrahams are hot on my heels & I have no time for more now.

N.M.   27/4/61

I'm too sorry about your father, he was such a dear, you'll miss him – especially having seen more of him lately. Yes, the English never fail to say, Far the Best for Him. If the person is old it's a merciful release &, if young, think how he would have hated growing old.

---

75. *Great Cricket Matches*, edited by Handasyde Buchanan, 1962.

We had a very exciting two or three days, though people in the know like Gaston, who was here, were never the least bit worried. Still, one heard tanks all right & there was enough display of force to remind one of the dear old war. Of course the English journalists all huddle together in the Crillon bar & work each other up until everything seems quite desperate . . .[76]

H.H.　5/5/61

. . . A book has just come out, edited by P[hilip] Toynbee, called UNDERDOGS. It has chapters on Unemployed, Diabetic, Homosexual, Impotent Husband, Uncharm, General Failure, etc. How careful one will have to be.

N.M.　9/6/61

. . . I haven't got a book to read but there doesn't seem to be much? As for a book to write (a more satisfactory occupation because I read so quickly) I haven't a clue . . .

H.H.　13/6/61

Chatsworth was the most intoxicating treat & I am still swooning from the beauties of it all. Every object as well as every prospect pleases. Even humans seem better than usual. How brilliantly Debo has done it all . . .

Raymond [Mortimer[77]] emerged from the same train at Chesterfield carrying a Gladstone bag & a typewriter which was reassuring for us as Anne & I had been turning into bags of nerves at the thought of arriving . . . A most beautiful

---

76. Paris was much affected by strikes at this time, as well as by demonstrations over the situation in Algeria.

77. Raymond Mortimer (1895–1980), critic and literary editor.

limpid evening which showed off prospects to full advantage as we strolled round a lake or two. It rained of course for ever after, but that did not matter too much what with the infinity to look at indoors . . .

N.M.   17/7/61   Venice

. . . I'm here for 2 nights & realize again how one can't know a house until one has slept in it . . .

H.H.   21/7/61

You've got quite a point, I think, about not knowing houses till one has slept in them. Does it apply to people too, do you think? . . .

Harold Acton has just sent me an advert for a new Italian drink called THE JOLLYCOCK: "what a curious name for a *soft* drink" he comments.

N.M.   18/8/61

. . . Delightful here as always in Aug. I hardly know a soul in the town. Just now the telephone bell for the first time in 3 days. "That you, Nancy – this is (sounded like) Samuel Whiskers." "Who?" I said timidly. "Samuel Whiskers of New York. I've got a little house in Versailles . . ." Well, the long & the short is he mesmerized me into saying I'd go down tomorrow by the 12.15. Do you think it's an American patriot luring me to my doom? I literally haven't the foggiest idea who it can be – he says I once wrote an article for him . . .

H.H. wrote a long letter in longhand while on holiday in Ireland. He and Anne stayed in Derek Hill's house in Co. Galway. After a sociable week with dinner parties every night, they stayed "in a converted railway carriage which

*overhangs the sea at Portsalon in N. Donegal. A gale is
blowing & the rain crashes against the carriage windows.
The view would be stunning if we could see it. The racks
are a great comfort. So splendid to be able to throw things
into them & not on the floor. I am going to start them
at Richmond as well as in the shop. [Nancy particularly
liked the idea of a rack slung across the children's room
downstairs.] At night we lie on joined bunks like effigies
on a tomb."*

H.H.   1/11/61

It's the dread first day of Christmas cards, so it's simply
been a case of up & down the via dolorosa [the shop's steep
staircase] sweating sequins & working out the fiddling
change instead of writing to you . . .

1962

... Horrid old Roger [Hinks[78]], baiting away. I said something about an autodidact like me. "Not much didact, I fear."
He's always holding up Alethea Hayter[79] as being a master of
syntax – I sometimes long to ask where it has got her, though I
admit that this is a vulgar thought ...

I've had a *shower* of gold from Alfred & rather think I
hardly need ever to write another ...

I've been asked to reply to a questionnaire from a Gov:
paper called Esquire (can there be such a paper?) If you had
your life over again, what would you like to do? A. Moon
about on a huge unearned income. Won't the Govs be surprised! Sharked, I guess.

N.M.   29/1/62

... The Carlyle [set] has arrived. WOE! 'tis the edition with
incomprehensible index I've already got. I could cry. But I
wonder if some clever person could explain the index to me –
Hinks perhaps. You look up Valoré. it says V p.19. You look
for Book V – there is NO page 19, it begins at p.54. If you're
me, you then give way to uncontrolled sobs ...

H.H.   31/1/62

... Sangorski [& Sutcliffe, bookbinders] seems in a dol-
drum. They refuse to mend books any more because they have

---

78. Roger Hinks (1903–63), art historian and author of *The Gymnasium of
the Mind*.
79. Alethea Hayter (b. 1911), historian and literary biographer.

so few apprentices. We are busy going to the dogs all round what with Monday tube & train strikes on top of post strikes. I am now the postman & have to take the parcels to Richmond [where the Hills had recently moved], & also the chauffeur as I pick up Handy at Earls Court on strike days. . . .

Handy has just come clattering down the via dolorosa with your letter containing dire Carlyle news. On top of tiny print the inexplicable index is too cruel & I feel miserable. Make Hinks do a complete new index as retribution for his terrible syntax rudery.

We had a young Irishman [Joseph Hone] here last week doing the catalogue. On the Monday night of chaos he disappeared without trace & hasn't been heard of since. Anxious relatives ring up – so wait for L'HORREUR de CURZON.

N.M.   4/2/62   Fontaines

Jamie wants to do a book of various essays I've written for the papers [published as *The Water Beetle*]. I suppose the critics would be fairly vile but it might make a few pounds, I daresay. The worst of it is, the pieces are all so short, as that is what the papers are now after.

H.H.   6/3/62

. . . I'm rather reeling after lunch with Dig [Yorke].[80] I thought that there was only going to be Dig, but there were Henry [Green], John Lehmann,[81] your Diana and Isobel Strachey[82] which made it all very fascinating, but I am not back till 3.15 & I think in disgrace with upstairs. Henry is

---

80. Wife of the novelist Henry Green [Henry Yorke] (1901–85), née Biddulph.
81. John Lehmann (1907–87), author and editor.
82. Isobel Strachey, first wife of the printer John Strachey, Lytton's nephew.

now like some wonderful ancient monument or unpredictable sage with his long brindled hair & green face & gaps in teeth & one doesn't know what or if anything will come next & one is kept in anxious though excited incertitude. He was funny about Evelyn. I swore I could remember his exact words to tell you, but of course I can't. It was something like "Isn't Evelyn himself the height of human folly?" & then, in no antagonistic way, went on to describe his last weekend with him when one of them had said, let's meet again & be friends. Henry had looked out of the window & seen Evelyn planting an ivy garden all wrong & Henry had told him so & Evelyn hadn't slept all night.

Then at luncheon the next day Henry said to Laura [Waugh], would it be all right for him & Dig to smoke in the middle? Laura said it would be all right for them but not for her, which Henry said he ought to have taken as a warning. So they lit up & then suddenly there was a crash as Evelyn swept up all the china from the table, saying he could not endure people who smoked at meals & they must have been mixing with Jews in New York (I gave an anxious glance at Lehmann who did seem a tiny bit pinker than ever), & after that he retired to his library & they never saw him again . . .

Have you heard how, when the Snowdons[83] were staying with the Frys[84] two weekends ago, they all asked themselves to lunch with the Lees-Milnes.* So the Lees-Milnes were up all night ironing doilies & then telephone rang at 10 & Alvilde said "You're not going to say you are not coming," & Jeremy said, "Oh no, we only want to know the way to Berkeley Castle where we are going to after lunch." So the L.-M.s went on ironing & then telephone rang again at 12.30

---

83. Antony Armstrong-Jones, Lord Snowdon, had married H.R.H. Princess Margaret in 1960.
84. Jeremy Fry (b. 1924) and his wife.

& it was Jeremy in a panic saying "she's taken a veganin & gone to bed." So only Jeremy & Tony came. When Tony left, he said, "I hope that Princess Margaret will come next time." . . .

N.M.   17/4/62

. . . I must send a [wedding] present to Hugh Thomas;[85] now what? Oh be merciful – I have overspent in a frightening way this year. That wretched Diana Coo[per] has debased the address book by giving cheap copies of it to all London. She is the limit . . . Philip Ziegler sent his book which is awfully good, I think it will succeed.[86]

N.M.   Good Friday 62   Aubrey Walk, W8

The folio is an awfully good idea. Should Sangorski put Hugh Thomas on it or will that double the price? Make it nicer . . .

Debo's son Stoker[87] has got v. bad reports at school & one says: He seems to think he's a character in his aunt's old world books. Debo couldn't think who this aunt was . . .

H.H.   24/4/62

I am having the blank book Thomased & they have promised to do it quick; I don't think even they can charge too much for a few letters . . .

Fidelity Cranbrook[88] came over to Snape one day [over the Easter weekend] & told me that Gladwyn Gladwyn[89] had

---

85. Hugh Thomas (b. 1931), historian.
86. Philip Ziegler, *The Duchess of Dino*, 1962.
87. The Marquess of Hartington; see biographical index under Devonshire.
88. The wife of Anne Hill's brother Jock, 4th Earl of Cranbrook.
89. Gladwyn Jebb had become the 1st Baron Gladwyn in the late 1950s.

rung her up & asked if he could come & see her. What he wanted when he came was to ask her if she thought that, on some [wedding] invitations, they could cross out the church part so that those people only came to the reception. F said of course NO – he must have separate invitations if he wanted to do that. Some people were ratty that they had to answer to a sec. Odd that high diplomats don't know better . . .

N.M.   21/6/62

. . . The smallest of the children here, aged 5, *minute*, dead white face from overwork like they all have, asked his mother if a school friend could come and spend Sunday "Il est formidable, premier en tout". So formidable arrived an even tinier shrimp with even whiter face & they spent the whole day under my window pretending to be Algerians & torturing each other. Oh dear, it was funny – what would the New Statesman say?

H.H.   11/7/62

. . . I was amazed by 10 Warwick Av [the Hills' previous home] when I had lunch there with Diana Coo[per] last week. Christopher Fry[90] & his wife & John Gielgud & Iris Tree[91] & a woman who seems to be called Magoosh were there. They talked about films I had never seen or even heard of, but Diana was nice & took me all over the house & showed me all the rooms she has knocked into one. I had resented it in imagination but she has done it very well & I was won over.

---

90. Christopher Fry (b. 1907), playwright.
91. Iris Tree (1897–1968), poet. Her biography, *Rainbow Picnic*, was written by Daphne Fielding, 1974.

N.M.   14/7/62   Venice

. . . I think it was brave of you to go to Warwick Av. – I could never go back to rue Mr. if I left. It sounded awful what she has done, I so loathe big shapeless rooms . . .

All the boys on the beach here wear a tiny wireless tucked in among their private parts – you *wouldn't believe* the din these things give out. It is a new & dreadful menace.

H.H.   13/8/62

I haven't written lately because shop life has been extra hectic. The packer took the wrong medicine so that his feet exploded and he has gone away for a month. On top of that Liz is boiling and bursting in Corfu and won't be back till end of month so that the rest of us, as you can twig, are pretty ratty . . .

I must quote you what H. James said in about 1870. "We are condemned to be superficial. The soil of American perception is a poor little barren, artificial deposit. We are wedded to imperfection. An American, to excel, has just ten times as much to learn as a European. We lack the deeper sense. We have neither taste, nor tact, nor force. Our crude and garish climate, our silent past, our deafening present, the constant pressure about us of unlovely circumstance, are as void of all that nourishes and prompts and inspires the artist, as my sad heart is void of bitterness in saying so." So you must make allowances for the poor things.

OH DEAR. Mrs Sebag-Montefiore's books have been sent to Lord Astor and vice versa.

H.H.   17/11/62

Your postcard about Great Hunger [by Cecil Woodham-Smith][92] was considered blasphemy by underdog whose bible the book is. "Far the best book in the shop by the length of a street." How many times have I heard that repeated to the costumiers as they are forced to take it away to make some wretched relation's Christmas an abyss of misery. My own tiny views, which are the same as yours are unheeded and drowned, but I feel them so strong that they make me treacherous. I have never so much wanted to come to the end of a book. I groaned through it for the sake of Cecil and the old shop tie . . . I talked to Raymond [Mortimer] about it at a party who felt very much the same, as one could read between the lines of his review. All others rave . . .

Anne & I & the Bucks [Buchanans] went to a party given by Jamie & Cecil at the National Book League in their bare neon-lighted rooms. We were neither trade nor fowl and it was not a very good party. Anne & Handy & Harriet & I were talking in a corner clump when, in a flash, Jamie was up on a footstool making a speech. Handy & Harriet & I know the signs & fled to the other end of the room like grease but Anne was taken totally unaware & found herself standing by Jamie's footstool with Cecil W.-S. the OTHER side of her and facing the whole congregation. It must have appeared to those who did not know Cecil that Anne was she. Anne put on one of her set frowning smiles at the floor. Harriet doubled up with audible shrieks and naughty Moll loved it too . . .

Sorry to say that your copy of HUNGER arrived looking like shredded wheat and it has had to be put in the charity tombola bin. If you sometimes whisper me some book you want, I will slip it off as a replacement.

---

92. *The Great Hunger: Ireland 1845–1849*, 1962, by Cecil Woodham-Smith (1896–1977), historian.

N.M.   21/11/62

. . . May I have Salzburger's book on De Gaulle please? You may charge me for it, said she generously with a venomous look at Dr Watson across the couch.[93] I've told Malcolm [Bullock] I see signs of revolt – gunpowder, treason & plot, barrels in the cellar. Don't blow up Evangeline [Bruce] who I hear practically lives there.

H.H.   23/11/62

I know that the boutique is exposing itself when I have to confess that it has never heard of, nor can trace in spite of great grubbings among publisher's circulars, a book on de Gaulle by Salzburger [it was in fact Sulzberger]. The only one on him that appears to have come out here lately is by Ashcroft. I don't imagine by the length of a street that Salzburger could be a gov? . . .

Malcolm was disgracefully tipsy yesterday after luncheon with Leslie Hartley. When the packer came up from the basement with a full sack, he shouted "Is Mrs Bruce in that?" & then began singing the Stars and Stripes. Shop swarming with govs of course.

PS Baroness St Paul has just ordered 20 Water Beetles.

---

93. Handy Buchanan was an expert on Sherlock Holmes.

1963

Malcolm Bullock suggested in December 1962 that H.H.
should adopt Handy. This is a tease that is difficult to work
out but N.M. thought it was a "simply wonderful joke". In
her letter of 4/1/63 she refers to Handy as "your adopted
son". "It's silly of D. T[elegraph] not to employ [him] for his
yearly book review. Whatever one may say, his account was
lively & amusing & original." She continued: "Reading
about Aunt Mabell [Airlie]'s book,[94] I see that in 1945 she
was reading [J. H. Shorthouse's] John Inglesant! Oh what
memories that evokes! Whose influence? . . . Happy N.Y. –
congrats on your new child."

H.H.   18/1/63

By A PICTURE OF ENGLAND you mean THE ANATOMY
OF BRITAIN[95] so I am sending it off to the Col. I am writing
this by one candlelight because of a power cut which THEY
say is going to happen more & more often. You can imagine
how that just makes it more of a quaint old Dickens store
than ever . . .

I had lunch with Malcolm today & heard all about the
especially flown foie gras [mentioned by N.M. in an earlier
letter] (by those mystery friends with names like Bugghard &
Fukker). Don't worry about reviews. You make them jealous
by being successful & established & what's more most of
them are too stupid to understand you.

PS Two men with guns raided the wine shop next door

---

94. Countess of Airlie (d. 1956), author of *Thatched with Gold*.
95. Anthony Sampson, *Anatomy of Britain*, 1962.

[Curzon Wine Co.] yesterday evening and made the man give them the till.

H.H.'s daughter Harriet married Tim Behrens in March. There are amusing letters about meals given by Tim's father – "he didn't want it to be EMOTIONAL and besides it would be UNPALATABLE", but H.H. did not explain why he was "full of fear" or report more than superficial, though entertaining, details.

H.H.   20/2/63

When Anne & I were away at Snape last weekend & Lucy was alone at Richmond with Mary Moore (sculptor Henry's daughter) a gang of 50 Richmond youth arrived & pretended Lucy was having a party (she had asked 2 or 3). They drank ALL the drink, threw rice over everything, had baths, lit a bonfire in the front garden & let off fireworks & probably stole my father's gold watch. Neighbours rang up the police who came in a black maria but don't seem to have taken any of them away . . .

Malcolm told how his daughter went to dinner & a theatre with the Queen. No body in waiting. No servants. Just helping themselves. The mustard had been forgotten & the Queen said "It's no good ringing in this house. Anything takes ½ an hour to come." So she shouted down the marble stairs. They went to ordinary stalls at an appalling farce & there was a drunk man two rows behind who started flicking paper pellets at them. The Queen didn't notice but Priscilla felt her hair becoming full of pellets. The detective made no disturbance as he decided rightly that the man would soon go to sleep. Malcolm was also funny about staying at Wilton with the Princess Royal[96] who didn't know how to go to bed

---

96. H.R.H. Princess Mary (1897–1967), only daughter of George V.

and kept them all yawning while she pulled some wool from an enormous sewing bag & knitted a tiny sheath which could only have been for a mouse's penis.

N.M.   5/4/63

. . . I'm coming over for the Ogilvy wedding,[97] partly to arm Mama up the aisle & partly, I must say, because it amuses me. I'm not asked to the Queen's party which is a mercy as it would have entailed a ball dress & I'm suffering enough over the wedding get-up. How lucky chaps are, to have no choice!

The present too is a puzzle. No good sending books, I feel sure. I wrote to Tessier & asked them to report some bits of silver but for £25 (which is what I paid for my rococo 1750 coffee pot) they have only got modern things which sound vile. So I'd better leave that until I come . . .

So see you round about the 24th. I'll come the day before, I expect, & leave on the Friday. My mother has hired a *white* car with woman driver – we shall be booed.

N.M.   9/4/63

. . . I shall give Harriet an object, not a book to be coals to coals.

Angus O.[gilvy] told my aunt he had over 5000 letters of congrat. As the Abbey only holds 8000, that makes 3000 enemies. Interesting.

N.M.   14/5/63   Inch Kenneth

My mother is failing – we are all here except Decca* – no idea for how long. Twice she has seemed to be going & then has rallied – we long for her to go in her sleep – she feels so fearfully ill. Of course she laughs too. She said if there's any-

---

97. Between Hon. Angus Ogilvy and H.R.H. Princess Alexandra.

thing in my will you don't like, do alter it. I said we should go to prison & she laughed tremendously.

She wants to be buried at Swinbrook which she says wd. be VERY expensive & hopes we shall laugh at her funeral . . .

For two days we were storm bound . . . We are 15 here, with the servants & nurses, nearly all, in fact all but two, women & children, & the boatman was quite overdone.

That's the news. I thought you might like to know, & perhaps tell any friends. There's a good deal of hilarity mixed up with the sadness.

H.H.   15/5/63

So sorry & sad to hear about your mother. I know what it is all like from own distressing experience – & all the pathetic lingering increases strain.

Nothing to tell you except little bits of shop. Harold Acton has been in here on most days during the last two weeks. He went back to Italy yesterday. He was eager to read your review of Auntie Nose [Violet Wyndham].[98] He commented, while dancing, "Cruel but Ah, so FRESH. How well she writes. She writes better and better." Those were the actual words. Then he told how Osbert Sitwell went with Violet to see Ada Leverson [Violet's mother] on her deathbed next door at the Washington Hotel. Only Osbert went in. She was making up her face and all she said was "Beware of Violet. She's up to NO GOOD." When Osbert came out, Violet asked him what her mother had said. Osbert answered "She said nothing. She was making up her face."

---

98. *The Sphinx and her Circle: A Biographical Sketch of Ada Leverson, 1862–1933* by Violet Wyndham (d. 1979), née Gore, wife of Guy Wyndham.

N.M.   19/5/63   Inch Kenneth

. . . Dreadful times here. She can't go, can't be comfortable. We all worry about our own death beds since 4 daughters don't seem enough, so what about those who haven't got any?

Of course the comfort of a *real* house, *real* fires, marvellous servants etc is beyond price.

H.H.   27/5/63

Thank goodness (?) it's over for you. You must have had a dreadful time & I am so sorry. I felt a deep pang myself as I always liked her and enjoyed her coming in here (which one can say of so few) . . .

When I came back from lunch Handy said, "There's a very interesting couple downstairs looking at the [Randolph] Caldecotts. They are not Beat because they look so virile." I found a woman in a dirty white cap & pink & white striped blouse and a man in a tweed fishing cap, mackintosh trousers and beard. I can't think why Handy thought them extra virile or why, if Beat, they were impotent.

Anne wrote to N.M. after Lady Redesdale's death. By 31 May N.M. was back in Paris ("I simply felt I must go home"): "Indeed it was very dreadful but also dramatic. Her last journey, over the water, bagpipes wailing, on a perfect summer night was one of the most beautiful things I have ever seen."

N.M.   8/7/63

I thought I would like to give Emma [Cavendish; her niece] the nucleus of a library of English classics – the sort I enjoy myself, viz. history & belles lettres. What have you got? We

can [try for] Macaulay, Carlyle (not co: works; Fred & Fr.
Rev.); Byron's Letters, Baskerville Prayer Book. I can't think,
my mind is a blank, do tell what you've got to give ideas. Of
course I could just give all those invaluable Oxford reference
books, but it wouldn't be so personal. The wedding is in Sept.

H.H.   [?/8/63]

Just whenever I think that I am going to sit down and write
to you, another Brute comes in. The last one said "Have you
got a paperback of [Axel Munthe's] *San Michele*? My sister
read it in Ryde and thought it such a good book." You must
tell me how much you want to spend on Emma & then I
will get really busy with Cliquery. Would the 2 vols. edition
of Byron's letters be all right, ed. Quennell, 45/-, or do you
mean more of a set? How about Horace Walpole's Letters,
Granville-Barker's *Prefaces to Shakespeare*, an anthology or
two like *The Spirit of Man* & *Texts and Pretexts*? Keats'
Letters, Aubrey's Brief Lives, Fanny Burney or do you hate
her? Trevelyan on Macaulay, Gosse's *Father and Son*. There's
always dear old *John Inglesant*. Anyhow, I'm sending you an
Everyman list which may give you an idea or two . . .

N.M.   16/8/63   Venice

That's wonderful – send all those & put in Ox. Comp.s to
Eng & Fr. Literature for good measure . . .

H.H.   25/9/63

Among the terrible couches which THEY have left on my
desk to deal with on my return is a plaguey letter from the
Duke of Wellington in which, among other horrors, he says
"some weeks ago I asked you if you could get a leather-bound
copy of the Memoirs of the Grande Mademoiselle. I have not

yet heard whether you know of the existence of this work." I have crawled as far as the London Library cat[alogue], but find nothing. Now please be angelic and send a postcard to say. I wouldn't ask if I wasn't sure that you could tell me straight. . . .

One of the reasons we took Lucy to Corfu [where they had just had a holiday] was that her friend Jane Asher[99] is in love with a Beatle and told Lucy that she would produce another Beatle for her. Just before we left, Lucy said "Isn't it splendid? Jane and the Beatles are coming to Corfu just the same time that we are!" They did turn up but luckily the other Beatle was already mated with a Liverpool hairdresser . . .

H.H.   17/10/63

Bloch [French bookseller] sent the Mlle. The D[uke] of W[ellington] came to see it and approved as much as ever he does approve and said he would have it but it must be furbished, so sighing with relief I sent it to the binder. It came back three days ago when by unlucky chance I opened volume five and found that a quarter of the title page had been torn out. It must have come from Paris like that – almost certainly must – so I wrote to the Duke and I wrote to poor Bloch (I had already paid him). I was hugely surprised this morning when Duke answered that a torn title page was a bibliophile's quibble and that he didn't mind as much as I did but no doubt the book would now be cheaper. So that has ended fairly all right considering, and I am very thankful to you and I only hope Bloch won't mind my letter which was in bad French but meant to be polite.

Two months ago a man came in with a small photograph album of Edwardian royalty. Handy told him to leave it and

---

99. Jane Asher (b. 1946), actress.

we would "see what we could do". It was of course immediately couched and utterly forgotten. The man came back one day early last week to ask what had happened. Handy told him that his album was worthless and that he would post it back to him. Three days later the man came in again at 11.31, just after Handy had gone for his dinner and said that it was disgraceful that the album had never been posted to him. I said how sorry I was but that Mr B had just gone out and wouldn't be back for an hour. "Do you mean to say," he said, "that YOU don't know what your partner does with valuable books like mine? I am staying here until it is found." I did a little grovelling and unearthed some mouldering object which I thought could be his and put it near the surface against Handy's return. When Handy came back he dived straight under the desk and, in his best dodgy manner, said how frightfully sorry he was that it had not been posted but that here it now was. The man went off appeased. The next morning was Saturday and I was in the shop alone when the man came in again. Never have I seen anyone so like an erupting volcano. Never in his life had he known such a case of sheer disgraceful carelessness. When he got home and unwrapped the parcel, he found that it did not contain his album but somebody else's. I must ring up Handy wherever he was and bring him back to the shop instantly. He would not leave until it was found and he would put his legal advisers on to us. In the meantime Lady Rosebery[100] had come in and was vastly enjoying herself. I said that Handy had gone to Yorkshire (he was really in Barkston Gardens, Earls Court). In the meantime the man had got down on the floor himself at couch level and was furiously groping while crumbling piles broke over him. In the end I could bear it no longer and told

100. Countess of Rosebery (1892–1987), married first to Lord Belper, then to the 6th Earl of Rosebery.

him to get up and that I would look. By enormous luck I found it under a smashed jigsaw, but the whole thing took one and a half hours. One of the worst episodes.

N.M.   19/10/63

Oh, Heywood, I'm *weak* with *screaming* at your letter. But also feel guilty about Mlle. The reason I hardly looked at it is when he [Bloch] said 100 francs, I felt sure it was too much for Dukey as at that time I imagined he wanted a copy to read himself – in fact I only reported it to show willing! Now we seem to have the worst of all worlds if he wants a reduction. Oh bugger, I AM so sorry . . .

I think the butler has gone mad – he sleeps over my room & I hear him shrieking with laughter, or singing, or doing a sort of Rumpelstiltskin STAMP in the small hours, or else having a bath. Probably only a matter of time before Osbert [Lancaster]'s illustration to my book comes true! He continues to supply dates etc at meal times when one's memory fails & did the Popes the other day which Ld. Macaulay said he never could, "I always get mixed up among the Innocents."

Osbert Lancaster's illustration to "Augustus Hare, 1843–1903", *The Water Beetle*, 1962.
With acknowledgements to the Estate of Osbert Lancaster.

'. . . to warn some high-born lady that her mad butler is approaching with an axe.'

H.H.   22/10/63

... All that I could read in a Ms. letter from Osbert Sitwell at Montegufoni was that Malcolm had written to him to say that THEY had asked him to be Prime Minister. What wonderful larks we could all have if only it were true ...

N.M.   25/10/63   Fontaines

... Abbé Girard, quite the nicest of priests, who came here, asked for *Voltaire Amoureux*, so I said to Mme. Costa what should I put comme dédicace. She said I think better put nothing or else when he is dead & they look at this books, he will be *compromised.* "You see you are such a beautiful young (sic) lady, it's not as though you were Mme de Pange." Can you wonder I like coming here! ...

H.H   12/11/63

The Wellington-Bloch-Mademoiselle ended not too bad as things end. I wrote to Wellington and said that because of half a title page being missing, I would charge him 10 instead of 12. Got back enclosed spiffing postcard [now missing]. I can't remember any more what I paid Bloch – something like 8 with post. Then there were repairs of frayed edges ... Anyhow I didn't lose and Gerry is graciously pleased ...

Now I must attend to that film star David Niven who wants a pair of prints 5½ feet long which have to be mounted on canvas and hung from slanting golden arrows – regency style.

N.M.   Christmas Day, 1963

... I've chucked the picture book – it bored me – and I'm going to do Louis XIV at Versailles. Hamilton is pleased & I am delighted – have done quite a lot already ...

*Deputé de la Seine
1 rue Bonaparte

7 RUE MONSIEUR VII.

GUTENEN 7005.

Would you send the Colonel* the II vol
of Deutch (is it called after Stalin?)
& he goes on about a book he wants
of pictures in country houses... I
haven't seen anything about it, but
you might know?

I've been offered 5000 dollars to
do an article on the poor little Royal
Dwarf. Didn't even answer. I
wonder who will!

It is 10 Warwick Av? If 12 (but
I'm thinking of Blor?) would you
open enclosed & correct?

Evelyn writes to say that as a
shareholder I ought to know that one
of your assistants puts the customers
off buying books (his) I feel entirely
on the side of the assistant if he is
referring to his latest effort...

I'll be in Sat morning. Have
you a frigidaire because if so I'll
bring some butter to save bothering
about a ration book (or is it
all off now? how about sugar?)

love from N

Hamishram says Jam! so your assistant
must advise people to keep their BTs for it!

G. HEYWOOD HILL LTD. ● **10 CURZON STREET LONDON W.1** ● **MAYFAIR 0647-8**
(Heywood Hill, Handasyde Buchanan.)

OLD AND NEW BOOKS

12 Nov.

Dear Nancy

Sorry I have been so long sending the stamps but Hal
kept me hard at it & there are the stained & mushroom-growing
couches on return. She said I was to send you her best love.
She was rather rheumatic (had been caught by a caller coming
backwards downstairs on all fours). Her M.F.H. was in bed
with shingles so I had nice rich comfortable meals often by
myself. There s a butler called Lovegrove & I was amazed to
hear Betty shouting at him 'If you can't make less noise, Lovegrove,
I'll have to buy you a pair of gym shoes. And, what s more,
if you must refer to me & the Colonel as Ma and Pa, please do
it out of my hearing'. I did'nt know one still could. Then
she whisked him off to give a dying peacock some brandy.

How did you feel about reviews, I wonder. Rather mixed
and muddled. Harold edgey as usual and Cyril quite funny.
Cyril was in here yesterday and said that he had had a nice letter
from you. They were controversial (the reviews) which is always
good for sales - as so is the way that you always make people take
sides. John Lehman says that he is doing it on the wirelss
on Sunday week. He has'nt read it yet - so I did my best to rightly
inspire him. He is doing Toynbee at the same time (he said he'd
enjoyed that but did'nt think it 'quite came off'.

I'm sending enclosed snap in case you have not seen it to cheer
you up. Supposing ONE changed, do you think one s parents would make
a group?

I long to hear how the signing went.

Love from

If you want more about Roberta I'll
send you Picture Post which has a
whole article and lots more splendid
snaps.

Letters from N.M. and H.H.

i

Top left: Handy and Mollie Buchanan at the bookshop. Top right: Mollie Buchanan and Liz Forbes on the shop steps. Centre left: Dorothy Cranbrook and Harold Acton in Naples. Above: Derek Hill. Left: Malcolm Bullock and Osbert Sitwell on the shop steps.

OPPOSITE Left: Heywood and Anne Hill, c. 1938. Right: Eddie Gathorne-Hardy. Below: Anne Hill and Osbert Sitwell at Renishaw.

Heywood Hill in his first shop at 17 Curzon Street, c. 1938.

Nancy Mitford in the drawing room at 7 rue Monsieur, Paris, 1960.

Left: Deborah and Andrew Devonshire with Emma, Stoker and Sophie, 1954.
Below: Left to right: Cecil Beaton, Nancy, Deborah, Pamela, Diana and Andrew Devonshire at Stoker's wedding, 1967.

OPPOSITE
Left: Cecil Beaton's jacket design for *Voltaire in Love*.
Right: Nancy and her garden at 4 rue d'Artois, Versailles, 1971. *Photo: Roger Gain, The Sunday Times Magazine*
Below: Ringo Starr, his girlfriend Maureen Cox (hidden), Jane Asher and Paul McCartney in Corfu, 1963 (the child in the foreground is unidentified).

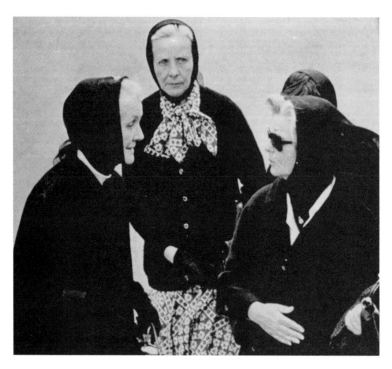

Above: Diana, Pamela and
Deborah at Nancy's funeral,
Swinbrook, 1973.

NANCY
MITFORD
Authoress
wife of
Peter Rodd
1904-1973

Right: Nancy's grave at Swinbrook
with her mole motif.

I turned on the Eng. wireless, hoping for a carol & got a song written by Vanessa Redgrave.[101] "I saw a bluck mun, hunging on a tree." I do wonder if the blacks go on about the white men *they* have slaughtered.

---

101. Vanessa Redgrave (b. 1937), actress and political activist.

1964

. . . That sounds a brilliant idea about you and Louis XIV and Versailles. Has all the sniff of a seller too, as hotbrick Hamilton must be twigging . . .

The last Christmas Eve moments at the shop were dire. We planned to shut at 4 to catch our train – to here [Snape], the Bs to the shires. At 3.30 a bevy of aristocratic drunken young came reeling in from the Turf Club. One collapsed on Liz's chair and said he would never reach Dorset by train – he was too ill – I must hire him a car (I did). Another said, what was that quotation from Yeats and why hadn't I got a Yeats and I must find out and he wanted to write it in Wuthering Heights. "What! not got Wuthering Heights . . ."

I agree about Eddie's little inadvertency.[102] I have suffered considerably from it. One side complaining that it is too short and badly printed and – as you point out – strikes too much on one ball. (Though, really, they all lapped it up, of course and the 200 copies sold in a flash.) The other side complained that I was too rapacious in demanding ⅓ for it and that I ought to have been more charitable to bankrupt Eddie. However, he gets almost £150 for almost nothing and never has a brochure been produced so quick to aid the indigent . . . Besides, I knew that if we did not get ⅓, it would be blasted by the undermaster.[103]

---

102. Hon. Edward Gathorne-Hardy, Anne Hill's brother, author of *Inadvertencies*, 1963; later reprinted as *An Adult's Garden of Bloomers*.
103. Another reference to Handy Buchanan.

N.M.   7/1/64

... I think £150 was quite enough when you think how Milton got £20 for P. Lost. Dear Fellow – I'd buy him like a shot if I could afford him.

PS I think all at the shop are dead. I asked for *Mary of Modena* by C. Oman, what a hope.

H.H.   5/2/64

... Oh dear, I'm in hopeless correspondence with John Banting about money which Brian Howard's mother has paid twice into the shop because he wants the twice. He also tells me I'm on a Brian list of people whom he wished "to control the republications of his writings", and will I start doing some republishing and controlling? Shall do a little soothing Clique work instead.

PS Awful thing is that something ought to be done about Brian. Many of his reviews were brilliant.

H.H.   9/4/64

Panic. Hysterico has written to me only today to say he is arriving next Monday for 4 days and will I book him a room "with a shower or bath in a comfortable hotel in the quarter where the publishers are." I have been desperately ringing up Bloomsbury places – the Ivanhoe, the Cora, the Kingsley to no avail. Finally I have got him a room with bath in the Howard Hotel, Norfolk St., Strand, for £3 a night. Will he faint at the price? Will he ever get my letter telling him?

Dotty of him not to ask me sooner. We MIGHT have had him at Richmond but couldn't be further from the publishers' quarter, could it? "Sorry to bother you, dear" he goes on, "It is my maiden voyage so I am afraid you must chaperon me." I thought Anne & I had ruined his maidenhead years ago.

N.M.   10/4/64

Oh poor Heywood (hysterico), I know what a dead BORE
that is. I'll try & get him on the telephone (what the Americans describe as call him – be called – it always conjures up a
card to me), but what between his love life & his work, which
never seems to take place at the office, it's not very easy – love
life doesn't take place at his very lovely home either, so where
does he spend his time? He's just finished translating [*The
Water*] *Beetle* which I'm calling *Voyages et Snobisme*. I think
brilliant invention of the Colonel's but hysterico, not having
thought of it himself, is luke warm.

H.H.   21/4/64

I am cliquing *Louis XIV Goes Camp* as well as the other
books you ask about. I see, in London Lib Cat., there is *The
Court of William III* by Grew . . . I will try to get a quotation
for a complete Lavisse, as well as for the Louis XIV vols . . .

Hysterico behaved disappointingly well. A 2nd letter followed hot on the first, before his arrival, saying he would face
coming to dinner at Richmond and that he was much tougher
now than he used to be, but would I tell Lady Anne that he
cannot touch anything acid – no fruit & not a hint of vinegar.
We already had young Heywood (my sister's son) and his wife
coming to dinner and, although they were fairly surprised by
each other, it was not disaster. Luckily young H is quite pretty
(though isn't it really elderly railway porters that Hysterico
prefers?) and he was thought to be "typically English",
though that may not have been a compliment . . . I believe
Anne & I lost considerable face by being found in our present
hovel . . .

Now you must tell me – with no sparing – everything he
told you about the visit. I can't help a weak spot for him – in
spite of paranoia – & he does make one laugh & he is quite a

tonic after suet pudding – though small doses do.

I heard a shepherdess' shrill pipe while banging this off in the basement, so went up and there were Cynthia Jebb with a Frenchwoman called Bethouart. They were being moderately tiresome about editions of Shakespeare and maps of London, but I soon whisked them off to the stationer in Shepherds Market where to huge relief nothing was more than 2/6.

N.M.   28/4/64

I've been very remiss, I know, about writing *re* Hysterico – partly work & partly that H. was so dull about it all, that's to say *pure love and praise throughout.* He thinks London is far more expensive than Paris. I've a good mind to write up about this because I always think so each time I go there, & yet the papers pretend the exact opposite. The fact is, when one is away from home, money *melts* . . .

I took Stoker to a lecture on Louis XIV illustrated by contemp: pictures on a screen & half way through he said he wished he was at Clacton [where the Mods & Rockers were revolting]. That's it.

N.M.'s next two letters – reproduced in Love from Nancy – *come from the Volpi Villa in Tripoli and from the Ostorog house on the Bosphorus. The latter "beats all for fascination" and Constantinople is "not at all the New York I had imagined . . . Am I not lucky [she was taken round the old seraglio etc. by her host]! The Turks so friendly & kind, so unlike those detestable Arabs among whom I will never set foot again, I swear." She asked the shop to send presents of her books to various Turkish friends.*

N.M.   Venice   19/6/64

. . . I saw a lot of Eddie [in Athens]. The toes are a worry, I fear, the friends very gloomy & they say he is awfully alarmed. If so, he puts a marvellous face on it. He went to bed for two days while I was there.

N.M.   1/8/64   Venice

. . . I saw Lucy for one moment looking well & lovely & with her foxy admirer, who is particularly handsome, I thought. The Desmonds [Guinnesses][104] have been topic A among Venetians – I must say one has seldom seen so *much* unbrushed hair, & Lucy shone out for having passed the comb if for no other reason.

Stoker & 16 friends are meeting at Viareggio today where they have taken a house from Rentavilla – goodness, just like in *Alfred*. One can't invent horrors fast enough these days. I really worship that boy & learn with sorrow that most of the 16 have motor cars which is rather more dangerous than going over the *top* my dear, as old Brian would have said.

H.H.   [10/8/64]

. . . I was intrigued that you had seen Lucy as, partly because of the [postal] strike, we never know where she was or who she was with. Who was the fox? Probably that man who calls himself the Knight of Glin[105] (Night of Sin, according to Derek [Hill], though Lucy in her last said that she was being "very chaste" and had not had to use those PILLS – boxes of which we spread all over her luggage, knowing how she loses things) . . .

H.H.   14/8/64

. . . Last week Handy sold a copy of FLORA LONDIN-

---

104. Hon. Desmond Guinness (b. 1931), architectural writer.
105. Desmond Fitzgerald, the Knight of Glin (b. 1937), art historian.

ENSIS to a customer who brought it back the next day saying that forty plates were missing (one of them was of a phallic fungus called STINKING MORRELL) which made us all shriek for several hours because the Lesbian dressmaker over the way [42 Curzon Street] who treats us as a library, never failing to return everything, is called Mrs Morell.

I swear that I have had *The Beauties of the Bosphorus* [ordered by N.M. after her visit to Turkey] most carefully collated and that all the pictures [steel-engraved plates] are there. I wish it had a more glamorous binding though it's what's called SOUND. You must return it in two years time if you hate it . . . Now, what is so dreadful, my oath has just been proved untrue. The girl [downstairs] has just told me that two pages ARE MISSING FROM THE BEAUTIES – so back it will have to go to Beach's at Salisbury, who I always thought so reliable (like US). I shall do my best to find you another before too long.

N.M.   26/8/64

Urgent. I find I've run out of exercise books. Also they are getting pretty muddling with their moles!! I suppose they don't exist with other covers by chance? Anyway pray send me four with moles in the oddest places anybody can devise viz. ⌐⌐ ⌐⌐ ⌐⌐ ⌐⌐ that ought to do. . . .

Eddie said something about selling the shop, I expect you've had enough by now but I also expect you'll miss it. The worst of a bookshop is it has to be all or nothing.

H.H.   31/8/64

I have just been to buy your four exercise books, and suffered from an unhelpful rude Ryman who would not admit to them being done in any other colour . . . Then I took them up those stone stairs to Sangorskis who were full of mole sympathy and promise to have them ready by tomorrow. I imagine you want to have those sent to [rue] Monsieur . . .

N.M.   1/9/64

Heywood, you're too good, I mean much too good, it puts one to shame. May I have book ⸤⸥ to Fontaines & the others here please.

Mr Hadfield?[106] Says he knows you. I've just had 2 hours with him. My book has got to be illustrated like Tutan Khamen & then I shall get £15,000 or possibly £30,000. Oh dear, Mr Hadfield, I'm so tired do go away, yes yes of course isn't it exciting it will spoil everything but never mind 8, or 16 millions people will see it & not a soul will read it. Go away now, that's a good Mr Hadfield & I'll send a synopsis as soon as I can . . .

N.M.   23/9/64   Fontaines

. . . I wish I'd asked your advice about the book. You see I was talked by my agent into making it an illustrated book done by [Rainbird]. I didn't care much for the idea but am told it is the new genre & people love it. Well, now Jamie & specially my American publisher had got second thoughts & say what do I really want? So I've weakly said I leave it to them. Peters [N.M.'s agent] thinks the picture book wld make far more money, than be a Penguin which people will read. Actually, if there is interest in the subject at all, my book is utterly different from [Vincent] Cronin's,[107] we hardly touch on the same things. Such an immense reign, well documented, makes that almost inevitable – each person does what interests him. Anyway I think it will be good which is the main thing . . .

---

106. John Hadfield (1907–99), editor of the *Saturday Book* and publisher.
107. Vincent Cronin, *Louis XIV*, 1964.

Will you really like retiring? I suppose so but it seems to make rather a long old age. But you could write a book about the shoppe, that would be *lovely*.

H.H.   29/9/64

. . . There are quite a lot of funny stories in that book of Eddie Marsh's[108] – not absolutely all of them intentional. His passion for Ivor Novello rather rivets one. Malcolm tells me that he [Eddie] used to call him IVORY BOY to his face & in front of others. One supposes that he (Ivor) was too vain and actory not to mind.

I think it's a very difficult dilemma about your book. I am sure it will sell whatever format it is published in. I should plump for the one which will make you most money.

I think that I shall LOVE retiring. I want to travel before too mouldered. I want to garden at Snape. Both Anne & I want to write (mine won't be publishable until most of us are dead but it COULD make money for one of the girls). However, negotiations are still not negotiated and tenterhooks are terrible (starting to cause tenters). I will go on full-time – anyhow for a few months – if needed – and hope to do catalogues, picture buying, book-buying abroad and doing time here when anyone is away – but it's not poss. to know until new regime starts.

N.M.   19/11/64

Have you faded out – what's up? Well, I have too, I'm awfully busy. . . .

Can you get me a complete Thackeray which the Col. wants for Xmas – how eccentric. Perhaps better quote, I don't mean from the works but the price.

---

108. Sir Edward Marsh, *A Number of People: A Book of Reminiscences*, 1939.

Between October 1964 and the end of March 1965 no H.H. letters survive. This was the period when he was negotiating to sell the shop to Henry Vyner.[109] The latter had just bought the majority share in Marlborough Rare Books, specialists in architectural books, and had very good social connections. H.H. cannot have known much about his reputation as a gambler or have realised that he wanted to milk the business rather than devote time and energy to it. It was inconceivable that he would be welcome to Handy and Mollie Buchanan, but Handy was to take over running the shop after many years as junior partner.

N.M.   2/12/64

. . . I always think Handy is like a villain in a Dickens novel; his heart is obviously *ink* under a sinister veneer of charm. I love the old creature but one has to see human beings as they are . . .

N.M.   16/12/64

. . . Better have a Thackeray with decent print, so the £18 one (sadly) cloth – oh yes. Would you send it to him at 1 rue Bonaparte, Paris VI.

---

109. Henry Vyner (1932–96).

1965

. . . However the present was a great success. Pierre, his servant, moiled up the stairs with sack upon sack of books & every one will be read I can tell you – he worships them. So it was worth getting good print.

N.M.   11/3/65

Thanks so much for your letter – all rather *sad* but never mind. I had one from Mollie saying tell all friends everything will still be nice in the shop . . .

I've finished the book but have engaged to write dialogues for a *lovely* film, for MGM (to make a nice lot of money & amuse myself, excellent combination). So from tomorrow I shall be busy again – v. difficult to explain to idle friends who all say but I thought you'd finished.

H.H.   27/3/65

. . . I felt extra QUEER last Monday morning – just before going to lunch with Malcolm at the Turf [Club]. He said, "let's go and look at Hors d'oeuvres" and then it was that I wondered if I should get through the meal. I didn't. I had to leave and have a nightmare journey to Richmond – brandy at Waterloo and desperately holding off Vesuvius . . .

In spite of many monsoons, I hope that I am piloting through the choppy seas of change without shopwreck. One thing that pleases Mollie is the thought of the place being done up. I hope that it won't lose its old-world charm, said jolly Jack Wilton[110] – staring at a couch or three. Think of the delightful months while the builders are in and the packing room has to be in the children's room . . .

N.M.   29/3/65

. . . You had better come here while Mollie is doing up the shop . . . Violet [Trefusis] *has* gone mad. She tried to bribe Gaston to get her the Grand X of the L[égion] d'Honneur by saying she will leave him her silver. Imagine how well that went down! (The Grand X is for people like Malraux).[111]

The film is too lovely. The last remains of Brit. empire, two forgotten islands, paradise, taken over by the Americans. (I've got some testing scenes between P.M. & President). Finally the Vice Pres. goes on a goodwill mission & is eaten. Their story, my dialogue. I'm madly enjoying it *and* covered with gold which arrives every week in bags.

N.M.   9/5/65   Cooleville House, Clogheen, Co. Tipperary

. . . I received a letter from a lady [Marie-Jacqueline Lancaster] who is writing about Brian, with one from him to you which made me *scream* (Sam finds you a toothsome morsel etc). I've sent her one or two anecdotes but my memory is awful.[112]

N.M.   28/5/65

. . . The film is finished & so is L XIV (being set) & I feel rather lost. Nothing to read . . . I've now got Voltaire's letters,

---

110. The Earl of Wilton (1921–99), who had met Heywood during the war and remained a loyal customer of the shop until his death.

111. André Malraux, writer and politician.

112. Published as *Brian Howard: Portrait of a Failure*, edited by Marie-Jacqueline Lancaster, 1968.

complete, 100 vols., in case any hope [of a buyer] – but I think I've said this before.

H.H.   4/6/65

Handy's claustrophobia – he keeps rushing into the street. It is in fact like the last act of Aida, except that there is sadly little love left among the entombed. I have settled into my mud cage and quite like it. It suits the pretty pictures. I am still kept in Coventry for most of the time and, though quite restful, I don't feel it a suitable place for nigh on 60.

N.M.   12/6/65

I've just had a vivid dream about the new bookshop & woke up crying! *Literally true*. It was huge, salmon coloured, tidy, radiators instead of flickering gas, & a dread young man got between you & me as we were discussing Brian & said this cuckoo-clock is Chippendale. Marie then appeared with my breakfast, greatly to my relief! . . .

The Army & Navy, having lost this die [for her writing paper], have very kindly made me a new one *gratis* – but now I hanker for a golden mole, instead of the address. Would this cost 10/- a sheet? I suppose so. My grandmother had a butler called John who went to her when they were both 20, as footman. Fifty years later, she said to him, telling of old times, why did you take my situation, John? And he said, because you were the only person who wrote on gold edged paper.

H.H.   14/7/65

Writing to you made me immediately hear of a Quintinye: INTRODUCTION pour les JARDINS, FRUITIERS ET POTAGERS, seconde edition, Amsterdam, 1692, 2 vols in 1; contemporary calf, gilt back, contents excellent. £17-10.

I have bought it anyhow so it will be here if you want it.

I had rather a pang last week selling a book which still had your pricing on it. A Grandville fables (It came back from the bookseller I sold it to with a note saying "Title and one plate missing," but that's nice because it's here still in memory of you).

I've been feeling rather a rotter that I sneaked about school to you in my last & wished I hadn't so you must ignore it all.

N.M.   14/7/65   Venice

How thrilling about the mole. I don't want the address & I want nice *white* paper, not too thick – Basildon Bond would do – double sheets. Mole in middle. When the time comes to send it, pause; I must get somebody to bring it – I had to pay £2 duty on some the other day. By the way, *never* send a book here – one has to go to the big P.O., miles away, armed with passport etc to fetch it. Ceci dit, if [Painter's] Proust arrives, I shall of course be pleased to have it. Ha! it has arrived, quite painlessly & I *am* pleased . . .[113]

Had a letter from the Foyle strikers saying, will I stop Foyles from selling my books. No I won't. I've got my living to earn.

N.M.   16/7/65   Venice

I'm thrilled for the La Quintinye. Don't send it until I get home . . .

N.M.   26/7/65   Venice

White Weave please, not horrid air mail. I rather hope it will go into my usual envelopes as such a bore otherwise, so

---

113. The second volume of George Painter's biography of Marcel Proust was published in 1965 (volume 1, 1959).

perhaps wait until Black Monday (9 Aug.) when I return to stair-rod rain in Paris . . .

N.M   13/8/65

. . . Mr Slade[114] is here & I've got the script of P of Love. If I rewrite the dialogue, as he kindly says I may, I think it might be quite successful but (under your hat) his idea of how people talk is more than peculiar!

Heywood retired from full-time work in the shop during the first few days of September. In May 1965 I had been told that the shop was looking for a young assistant and I was interviewed by Handy after work one evening. His first question concerned the connection I had with Heywood Hill. I explained that his nephew Heywood was married to my first cousin Jenny. "So there's no blood in it?" "No, just a connection by marriage." "If the answer had been yes, I would have asked nothing further." This might have revealed the depth of his feelings against the Hill family, but I did not realise until I started working there, three days after Heywood's departure, that I had deliberately been kept away from him. While Handy was away after Christmas, I asked Heywood if we could share a drink after work. When we were sitting in The Grapes in Shepherd Market, he said, "I wondered how long it would take you to talk things over."

He continued to work two days a week for a year after his official retirement, banging away on his ancient typewriter in the Print Room, taking prints to the framers in Seymour Place and, very occasionally, appearing upstairs when one of his friends asked for him.

---

114. Julian Slade (b. 1930), composer of the musical *Salad Days*.

N.M.   25/9/65

I've been staying with Harold [Acton] – perfect heaven, everything I like best. One wakes up in a room longer than the Chatsworth drawing room with sun streaming onto the bed so that one has a comfortable sun bath. Then the art, both in the house & the galleries, knocked me silly. We lunched & dined out in wonderful villas – with such gardens. Oh Italy, there's nothing like it . . .

Now I'm here correcting my proofs, trying on clothes (having counted my chickens as per) & getting new covers for the drawing room . . .

N.M.   4/10/65

. . . Your letter – I read "the packer left because of his girl friend's adoration for Maudling."[115] I now see "girl friend's abortion (so muddling)" which is much less dramatic, do admit.

N.M.   2/12/65

How's everything? Are you at the shop or have you chucked it? Is it true the new boss has gone bankrupt? . . .

Could you be a saint, if you write, & tell me the best English art mag.? Apollo? (It's for the Col.) and saintlily tell the address so that I can write. I want to worm away from the bookshop now that you're out of it, so wld. rather not do it through them – unless you say I should.

N.M.   4/12/65

Here is the dear little creature [the golden mole on her

---

115. Rt. Hon. Reginald Maudling (1917–79), Chancellor of the Exchequer the previous year.

writing paper] – very much like, I now see, King Clovis's *toads*. I'm simply delighted with him. My old Miss Mitford[116] writes to say "I am madly in love with your Mole. When I was a child the peasants called them cunts, a word one never hears, now." *She's* not in the Tynan set!

H.H.   12/12/65   Snape

I wasn't sure about which art mag. is best so have been writing to ask the wiser. They say that Apollo IS the best . . . The Burlington Mag. is also good . . .

I long increasingly to be down here all the time. I expect I shall be finally totally sacked by the shop next autumn.

---

116. N.M.'s aunt Iris Mitford (1879–1966), sister of her father Lord Redesdale.

1966

. . . Appropriately a depressed man has just been into the shop & said "I've come to mend the starter on your boiler." Of course, there are no starters or boilers – even under the new reign. It's a relief to tell you, however, that occasional yore-like things do happen – in spite of the now spick and spannery. There was a furious letter from a gov. last week asking WHY the £40 worth of old books which he bought last September had never arrived. I was able to be splendidly smug about it as had been in Ischia at that time and, with my couch eye, I spotted them at once far under the new boy's desk. I showed them to Handy who pulled them out but, because they were deep in filth, which would be bad for his breathing, he gave them immediately to Liz who let out one of her deafening raspberry shouts . . .

I had a letter this morning from Pam [Jackson] in her Buhl.[117] She says will I get for her that "thrilling old children's story of forests, pigs, hermit, robber barons & good barons and the cruel old grandmother."

N.M.   2/2/66

. . . Some poor wretch has been jumped on by Jamie (truly nothing to do with me, I tried to restrain him) for copying out great hunks of Pomp. I must say it has to be seen to be believed – what a funny thing to do . . .

---

117. The address of N.M.'s sister Pamela Jackson was "im Buhl, Mougins, Switzerland".

The mysterious Rainbird stands over me, pen in hand, &
offers me the whole gamut of the fancy dress ball for my next
book, Charles II, Catherine the Great & now Casanova. I
simply won't play – not inspired.

H.H.   10/2/66

. . . Osbert Lancaster has just been in and says that your
plagiarist is an old starving cripple in a garret and that now
there is nothing ahead for him except the geriatric ward in the
workhouse.

*N.M. felt guilty about this: it looked as if, as a successful
author, she was "trying to down the poor & wretched." She
had known nothing about it until "a young lawyer brought
a thing to sign saying Pomp was [my] unaided work." The
lawyer told her she could have at least £350, to which she
replied that there was "no question of money," but she would
prefer that it shouldn't cost her anything. The publishers of
the plagiarising work, Frederick Muller, were much to blame
and N.M. hoped that Heywood would put it about that her
intentions were "pure, really for once, quite pure."*[118]

H.H.   26/4/66

You must have been very sad about Evelyn [Waugh].
Another of those blows which happen too soon. It's always
worst it being one's own age. . . . Handy went to the Service
and sat with Betjeman, Driberg, Fulford[119] and Patrick
Kinross.[120] He said that it went on for an hour. All that
Catholic muttering.

---

118. The book was *Painter, King and Pompadour: François Boucher at the
Court of Louis XV* by Ian MacInnes, 1965.
119. Roger Fulford (1902–83), biographer and editor.
120. Patrick Kinross (1904–76), traveller and writer.

Anne and I have moved from Richmond so that now our permanent address is Snape Priory . . . the motion of course was hell. The van broke down when it had only gone a mile or two and all our things were strewn on the North Circular road in driving damp and arrived three days late at the same time as a herd of grandchildren. I have switched my shop days to Mon. and Tuesdays so that I only have to spend one night in London.

Derek [Hill] appeared today looking enormous. Handy annoyed me by saying to him, "You get younger every day while the rest of us get older." Liz & I shouted at him, "Speak for yourself." I have to keep changing my seat as Handy is being photographed by the Press. There is a full-page history of him in the Evening Standard on Friday.

This profile by Maureen Cleave caused considerable upset, failing to mention Heywood's name at all, or that he had recently retired.

N.M. 26/4/66

Oh Evelyn – I mind.

Like you, I am up-sticking, to Versailles where I have found a dear little old house which I can afford . . . The rent here has suddenly doubled & there's nothing to stop it doing so again. I really long for something of my own in which to fall down dead. Debo's children anticipate this happening any day now . . .

N.M. 9/5/66   Lismore Castle

That interview with Handy, sent by faithful Mrs Law,[121] made my (& Debo's) blood boil. Not one word about you.

---

121. Joy Law, who worked for George Rainbird.

"The first time Evelyn W. came into the shop." Evelyn had lived in the shop for years before Handy ever went there. Honestly he is the original human cuckoo – I loathe him – though I must admit he has a certain sultry charm . . .

H.H.   16/5/66   Snape

Anne & I couldn't help feeling very pleased by your boiling blood. Such a winter wind as the artful dodger blew in his article was chilling but it made me thankful that I have been able to escape in time. . . .

How splendid and exciting about Versailles. The upheaval may be frightful and all that not knowing to do with what one has kept . . . I didn't want to leave Warwick Av. so the move to Richmond was hell but every day here I am more pleased about it. *Here* is a hideous house outside but inside is quite pleasant and the real thing is its surrounding oasis of trees and nightingales and overgrown sleeping-beauty garden. . . .

The woman who is writing the Brian Howard book has lent me the typescript hoping that I will suggest the prunage, I am reading it through riveted but with no pencil and see it would take me 3 months at least and haven't time to do that for love. . . .

N.M.   22/5/66

. . . Isn't it extraordinary the way they turn on the dead in England now? I would like to write up & say how terribly kind Willie [Somerset Maugham] always was to me from my earliest & dullest days – so was Syrie [Maugham] incidentally. I would love to know where all the jackals got the idea that Evelyn was a social climber of low origin. How well I remember his first mother-in-law Lady Burghclere (who was learned & the sister of Lord Carnarvon the Egyptologist)

saying how pleased she was that her daughter should marry
into such a good literary family. Oh well – people get everything wrong & are paid to do so & one sees the same thing
with historical figures – nothing so true as give a dog a bad
name.

H.H. 21/6/66

Now it's Malcolm [Bullock]. Too sad and depressing for
words. Quite half one's shrieks have gone for ever. He was
such a tonic – such an agreeably medicinal one – purging and
deflating one's little sillinesses and bringing one bumping to
earth – but nearly always so that one laughed. I shall miss him
dreadfully.

What is so horrible is that I was the indirect cause of it all. I
had told him about the Edith Sitwell Memorial concert
during the Aldeburgh Festival and urged him to come & got
him a ticket & a room in an Aldeburgh hotel and a ticket for
another concert the night before. He was to drive himself
over, leave his car here & I would take him on. I had been
uneasy about the 70 miles that he would have to drive himself
& I had tried to persuade him to take the train to Ipswich . . .
but he wouldn't. Telephone went after lunch. It was the first
man at the accident who had gone up & spoken to Malcolm,
& Malcolm had asked him to ring me up at once to say he
would not be arriving. The man said that Malcolm did not
seem badly hurt but that an ambulance was taking him to
Ipswich hospital. His car had skidded while he was going
round a roundabout on the Ipswich by-pass. The car behind
had slightly hit him and his car went off the road into a lamp-
post. I dashed into Ipswich and found him in the casualty
ward lying on one of those trolleys and waiting to be exam-
ined by the doctor. He said that his chest and back hurt
slightly but he did not appear in any major pain – only gave

an occasional little grunt & his usual blowing. The doctor came & said he could go home. We even debated whether he might still come on to Aldeburgh. He wanted me to ring up his man to come & drive him home but that would have meant about two hours more of waiting so I told him I would take him. He was strangely silent on the way back which I decided was shock & downcast & that feeling of disgrace & wondering if it was really one's fault after a motor accident (he said that the brakes had failed but they hardly ever do fail). He didn't want to go to bed when we got to Middlefield. His couple seemed properly solicitous & were going to ring up his doctor & I felt that he wanted to be alone – so I left him. I rang up the next day and the man said that the doctor had thought that Malcolm ought to go into a nursing home for about a week. After I left Snape for the shop yesterday morning, the man rang up Anne there and told her that Malcolm had had an operation & never recovered consciousness. I have not discovered what the operation was for. If ONLY I had rung him up & told him to come the Newmarket way which I knew was better than the Ipswich way. If ONLY I had rung up & said the roads are frightful, come by train. IF . . .

PS There is one rather hideous thing which I have to tell. A book has just been published called MAYFAIR. By R.[eginald] Colby (friend of Harold Acton). In it he mentions the shop and then he mentions you and brings up that story "a little less DARLING and a little more ATTENTION please" – without going on to tell of your magnificent work for the store . . .

Following extract is from a letter from Brian [Howard] to his mother. "As long as children are protected, it really doesn't matter going to bed with a lamp-post." I rather liked "So many problems resolve themselves for the clever-weak". I consider myself a clever-weak.

H.H.'s account of Malcolm Bullock's death did not reach N.M. for some weeks. She felt that "at 75 it's not as tragic as Eddy [Sackville-West], Roger [Hinks] & Evelyn, all at 60"; it had been a sad sequence.

N.M.   Athens 22/6/66

Oh Heywood, I'm *minding*. What happened? He seemed so well & cheerful such a few days ago in Paris. Mark [Ogilvie Grant][122] shouted the news through the bathroom door, I see he doesn't a bit realize what a great friend Malcolm was, so am controlling myself as one doesn't want to cast a gloom. I can hardly believe one will never see that quizzical affectionate look again . . . You must be miserable . . .

I'm reading Evelyn's letters to me, between tears & laughter. Heavens he was a *TEASE*.

H.H.   28/7/66   Clayton Manor, Hassocks, W. Sussex

. . . I'm away from Snape for ten days so your letter followed me to here . . .

They tell me that Deirdre Connolly[123] got drunk at the Astor ball and flung her bag at Margaret Vyner[124] who was dancing with Alan Ross,[125] but her aim was so bad that it first hit Cyril on the ear and then Jonny Gathorne-Hardy on the head (surely it must really have been one or the other.) Perhaps she threw it twice. Jonny said that Cyril said wearily something like, "Does one have to stay and watch one's wife or can one go to bed?"

---

122. Mark Ogilvie Grant (1905–69), a close friend of N.M.
123. Cyril Connolly's second wife.
124. Wife of Henry Vyner, the new shop owner.
125. Alan Ross (1922–2001), writer and editor of *The London Magazine*.

N.M.   28/8/66

I got back to 23 days of unforwarded mail & have only now ploughed my way through the most urgent of it. Never saw such an awful sight! Perhaps the funniest letter was from Monty[126] saying he hopes I will send him my book as he wants to possess all my works. I suppose he doesn't know about bookshops.

Robin [McDouall]'s[127] idea [a party at the Travellers' Club for H.H.] is a flash of genius. Oh how I would love to be there but you know what it is with me, I droop at parties – can't stand more than half an hour. . . .

Will Handy go to the party dressed as a crocodile?

On the day of the party N.M. sent a telegram to H.H. at the Travellers: HAPPY NEW LIFE LOVE NANCY.

In mid-October she received a long fan letter from John Creuseman, "the only reliable journalist I have ever met". One paragraph read: "I trust that the Sun King beams away royally: that rogue Handasyde Buchanan to whose shop I regularly go – partly for the pleasure of seeing him bully his customers –, when asked by one of them how the book was faring sighed . . . & said of its sale & success 'it's going disgustingly well.' At that point I caught his eye like Mr Speaker & later on when we were talking alone & knowing that we know each other, Handy hastily confided that he had told you himself he had not read it. Not but what hearing him with many another customer, one would believe him . . ."

She found such mischievous anecdotes of "the old brute" irresistible.

---

126. Field Marshall Lord Montgomery of Alamein (1887–1976).
127. Robin McDouall (1908–85), cookery writer and Secretary of the Travellers' Club.

N.M.   17/10/66

... [Geoffrey Gilmour] & I grieve & mourn that we shall never see you. It's really too awful to think of. I hope at least you are writing the book to end all books about the Shop.

I must say I understand leaving a town & can't wait to get into my house [in Versailles] & *breathe*. The air is completely different. I go constantly to grub about in the garden but don't expect to be installed before 1967.

I went to Frankfurt Book Fair & felt *very sick all the time* while doing things like being polite to 200 German booksellers in an ogre's castle at 10AM while the g.b.s swilled champagne & ate cocktail food. Don't! ...

H.H.   27/10/66

Found your letter with fascinating enclosure from J. Creuseman on return from Ireland. ... If you don't look out I'll write you an American letter ALL about TINTS [as in autumnal tints]. The first night in Ireland we stayed with the Moynes[128] at Knockmaroon. Bryan, unalterable, was standing outside the front door as we arrived, boat-battered, before breakfast, and, almost at once, handed us EACH a typescript of a play in verse, founded on Greek myth, which he had just written, with blank paper & pencil for comments. We were appalled to hear ourselves agreeing to go to church with him. A sycophantic parson who bowed to Bryan and called him M'Lord as well as asking us to pray for the Institute of Horology ...

My copy of the S[un] K[ing] arrived just before leaving. I thought it would suffer en voyage, but when I got back looking forward, Eddie had bagged it. He has just finished it

---

128. Lord Moyne (1905–92), first husband of Diana Mosley, and his wife, Elisabeth.

and said "I almost want to write to her." You could not have higher praise. He never flatters and he hardly ever praises. "I enjoyed it very much indeed, my dear." Then he said how hard you must have worked.

We stopped to look at the Ladies' house at Llangollen.[129] Only just in time because it has every sort of worm because of them [the Ladies] lining the rooms with old chest lids. "The Dykes of England should subscribe to save it" bellowed Anne in front of amazed workmen. . . .

N.M.   5/11/66

Most gratified by Eddie's remarks as he is *one who can read*. So rare.

I seem to read a book every day, it comes awfully expensive. How are you going to manage or have you got a life abonnement to the shop? People are already beginning to say the shop takes no trouble any more & I can't say there has been any response to my appeals for Scott's Life of Buonaparte. . . .

---

129. Sarah Ponsonby and Eleanor Butler; see Elizabeth Mavor, *The Ladies of Llangollen: A Study in Romantic Friendship*, 1971.

1967

N.M. moved to 4 rue d'Artois, Versailles, in February 1967.
There are no letters in the early part of that year when she
was arranging the house and garden. Meanwhile, H.H. was
sinking into the delight of retirement, but "after almost a
year I am still not sunk. All those PAPERS are still floating
about in their couches undocketed and, until I have done
them, I cannot begin what work I want." In the same letter
he gave a graphic account of Anne's brother Eddie Gathorne-
Hardy's domestic habits. He had come to Snape for the
winter and displayed all the self-indulgent habits of a
giant sloth.

H.H. 16/2/67

. . . About the table which you so kindly offered, I am in a
dilemma which I think I must TELL or else will seem such an
unthankful rotter. Brass tacks are that my nephew (who told
he was coming to take it away) says that Mollie says that the
shop bought that table from you (in dim past, I suppose). I
went into the shop the other day and told Handy that I would
write to ask you if you remembered. I don't remember at all
but Mollie's memory is probably v.g.. Handy said that I must
NOT write to you but that the shop had better give me the
table. The thing really is, however, that I don't want the shop
to give it me (I didn't think of that till after I had left Handy &
appeasement).

What I'll do is this. If you don't remember selling, I'll take it
and know it's from you. If you now do remember, I'll not take
it. I like it but I shan't sob if I don't have it. It's your thought
that counts (it really does). Whatever happens, I beseech you
not to write to either of them. My relations with Handybag

are, I think, better just now and I long not to do any buggering. It's so dire that anything to do with the shop becomes a torture.

H.H.   6/5/67

Anne & I were driving to the Lees-Milnes from here and we were wanting some lunch and we didn't know where to stop. Then I saw a signpost which said Swinbrook and I knew that, in proper reverence, we must stop there. The little pub by the river (The Swan?) seemed delightful, and they were ever so civil and gave us some edible food. After lunch we thought that we would look at the church. First I found myself staring at Bobo's grave and then, inside, at Tom's tablet.[130] It made one sadly think . . .

We seemed to be getting to Alderley too early so we dawdled on & looked at Berkeley which we thought was fairly glum. It was Easter weekend so even the tiny lanes were full of grannies in cars who made Jim sick by being there. One stopped to ask him the way and he told her to go straight home. . . . I like staying there and don't much mind the cold and lack of drink which some complain of. It is civilised and everything so pretty to look at. If only Alvilde could make herself a little less jangled – they grate on each other like emery. Of course one gets what-for if any mud speck visible (so different to here where this morning I found an old rusk and brassiere in the car) and merciless harping about getting her seats and a bed for the Aldeburgh festival. . . . Alvilde, on latest p.c., says that you will be staying there soon on way to P[ursuit] of L[ove]. That makes me jealous – I mean that WE are not on the way (of course, it's one of the great delights of here that it's on the way to nowhere). Wouldn't you think of it

---

130. See note 9. Swinbrook, Oxfordshire, was the Mitford family home.

sometime and kill Gladwyns with same stone – please? Cynthia [Jebb] has asked us to dinner tonight to meet the [Francis] Watsons. . . . Before going there, we have to go to a tenants' party at Glemham which Jock and Fidelity are giving because of the engagement of Gathorne (their eldest) and Caroline Jarvis.[131] They were engaged last week and are to be married in a registry office next Tuesday though really they have been on a brink for several years. Anne and I are delighted because we like Caroline v. much and we believe, in our coming dotage, she may bring us custard and flannel. . . .

There has been no more TABLE talk and as my last letter (two months) to Handy has obviously been couched, I shall let it sadly slide. While typing this letter, a swallow has flown in at the window . . . Eddie is back in Greece. Says the coup [by the Colonels] was a great bore, my dear. "I had to be in by 7 on two nights running." Think of that . . .

N.M. 11/5/67

Your lovely letter – how I screamed at all the stories – specially Jim and go home. He's getting to be awfully like Uncle Matthew which is drole when one remembers U.M. turning him out into the snow for being red. . . .

The Watsons are still much in my life because the Wrightsmans[132] have become great, almost bosom, friends. Old Charlie isn't one of those oily American dourlings but extremely tough & such, & I can get on with him. He can take teasing like an English person.

P. of Love. Don't know what to think. I go to Bristol next week for the rehearsals & shall know more by then, too late to say stop. I've cleaned up the dialogue to any extent &

---

131. The present Earl and Countess of Cranbrook.
132. Charles Wrightsman (1895–1986) and his wife Jayne, collectors and benefactors.

taken out all references to class. One song went: I do want my girl to be a lady wh: I changed to I do want my girl to be a half wit. Do hold your thumbs. I'm rather worried about money because I can see living in a house not a flat is very much more expensive. The net result of Sun King topping Smith's trade list for months is that I owe Rainbird £1000. Ay de mi.

N.M.   10/7/67   Venice

. . . I could hardly bear to leave my new house – I'd dug up the whole garden & sown with poppies & cornflowers & the result was STUNNING. I suppose I shall get back to a sort of hideous flowerless tangle.

H.H.   24/7/67

. . . THE TABLE. It has been released. So now I can be truly and deeply thankful. Such a splendid memento of a happy partnership which steered through all the rocks and mice.

I had a letter from Osbert [Sitwell] and in it he says "Talking about rows, Handy had the temerity to send a message by my nephew Reresby[133] to say how unspeakably hurt the shop was not to continue supplying me with books. As the object of the row was for them to feel hurt I feel very pleased."

H.H.   4/11/67

Cynthia rang this morning to say that you are coming to stay with her. She has asked Anne and me to lunch one day and Eddie on another. Splendid. I should also have liked to get you over here – just so that you can see our trou. . . . You mustn't expect a sweet Priory. It's shapeless, red brick, 1870

---

133. Sir Reresby Sitwell (b. 1927), who inherited Renishaw from his uncle.

in gone-to-seedy ground. But if you remember Hinkabelle [Roger Hinks]'s saying after his own visit "Don't go there. All you get is watered wine in a ploughed field" you must NOT be put off. . . .

The young man who now works in the shop is staying here for the weekend. (it mustn't be discovered or he will be given hell or even sacked). He says that the reprint of *Ladies of Alderley* is selling very well.

N.M.   9/11/67

. . . Yes, well, when Cynthia said, what neighbours do you want, I suddenly remembered that Snape is near – I can't think of you & Anne as neighbours somehow, a word which evokes my father throwing stones at Majors and their hideous wives . . .

Lesley Blanch said, who is that rude woman at H. Hill's? I said she isn't rude, she's got a loud voice. "She was rude to me & rude to E. Box'[134] . . .

I've been busy of late – re-doing up to a point *Pompadour* which Rainbird are to bring out as a companion vol. to *Sun King* – rather splendid as I seem to be going to make a bit more money very painlessly. Also I've written an article which makes me laugh, but perhaps nobody else, on Tam & Fritz – in other words Carlyle & Fred the Great. It took almost as long as writing a book would have.

---

134. Mrs Marston Fleming, naive painter and close friend of Lesley Blanch.

1968

. . . The B. Howard broadcast is at last over (I shudder whenever I think that I forced you and Cynthia to listen to my piece). They cut most of what Eddie and I had written (Eddie's was mutilated), as expected, but the result was not so awful that I feel I must emigrate . . . The actual recording of Eddie and me down here was a shriek, but I can't remember if that had already happened when I saw you. I had to ask strangers on Saxmundham platform if they were called Pocock, for that was the name of the man the BBC had sent down. A shakey old thing of my age. Eddie very cross because his train arrived at 11.30 and the engineer from Norwich wasn't coming till 2.30. However Shakey was keen on the gin and Anne cooked a good lunch, so time passed easily. As soon as I started my ordeal, after engineer had erected his mike, the table began to vibrate (one castor missing) and then a low hissing noise arose (poor Anne had a desperate time switching off washing-up machines and night-storage heaters), so there were constant interruptions and beginnings-again . . .

H.H. had just heard that the English Opera Group planned performances in the Chapel at Versailles of Britten's Burning Fiery Furnace *and* Curlew River, *for early May. He suggested that he might get tickets for N.M. and Geoffrey Gilmour, not supposing they would like either piece, but thinking that the first would be safer – "in Curlew River, an elderly man is dressed as a Japanese mother, & I'm afraid you might shriek." There was much discussion over the next few weeks as to where H.H. would stay and with whom.*

N.M. 21/1/68

. . . I've just had a *vivid* dream about Osbert [Sitwell] looking young, well & golden haired. Oh alas! But I had a letter saying he is much better & going to Venice . . .

Of course I missed the broadcast on Brian – Robin [McDouall] says you were wonderful (I've just read it in The Listener – it makes me die for the book).

I got Maggs's catalogue of Voltaireana. Old books are cheap. You can get contemp. copies of nearly all V.'s works for about the price of a Brian! . . .

H.H. 13/2/68

. . . I've really had too much of Brian by now. This morning, if you please, I had a letter from somebody who says he was with me at Eton and knew Brian and would I have lunch with him. He also says that he has got a book "which unfortunately was flung into a damp attic while I was in the Grenadier Guards". He says he's going to bring it into the shop (doesn't know I've gone) for me to dry.

You know there's a very great movement on here now called BACK BRITAIN. Lucy couldn't think what to take her brother-in-law's brother who'd had a fearful motor smash, when she visited him in hospital – until she found a little badge with BUGGER BRITAIN printed upon it. I know I shouldn't be telling you. You'll be going and ordering a whole lot for when you next visit stately homes.

N.M. 16/2/68

If you don't send me a Bugger Britain Badge, we are on non-speakers . . .

All the with-it French pansies are reading Brian, thank God I *seem* to have behaved much better than I really did (I fear), so they think I was quite heroic for the Cause & ask me to things. . . .

Love to Anne & to l'Honorable [Eddie Gathorne-Hardy] or has he flown to the arms of the Colonels?

H.H.   21/2/68

. . . Hon. is still with us. Doesn't flit till April.

Oh mercy. The B.B. badge. I've told Lucy of your ghastly threat but she's just off to a Tibetan monastery in Scotland and I haven't much hope. . . .

H.H.   7/4/68

I have got my ticket now for Paris . . . I feel a bit of a rotter deserting Anne as there are such terrible heaps (couches) to deal with here. You may have heard that her mother died – 3 weeks ago tomorrow – and now we are in the awful aftermath of wills and divisions (FIVE greedy people – not including greedy me). Most of the furniture – and the chattels – which belonged to Mama has got to be sold, so there's always a ferreting auctioneer. Everything is smashed, of course, but the ferret says that even smashed things sell now. I suppose because Trade has got so damn good at gumming. They gum up a cabinet in the most concealed way and then it falls to bits on the customer when he puts it in his house and turns on oil-heating. We have managed not to quarrel so far (except one day when Anne & I & Ed were having lunch together and they began on one another about jam). By some blunder we'd taken Ed's apricot (brandy-flavoured) for breakfast & he was very cross. I began, infuriatingly, shrieking – it was so funny – though I was a bit scared I must say, they were both so flushed and Ed was thumping the table until Anne pulled it apart (those iron things falling out) so that three plates and one sauce-boat fell through the gap. She was raising the dish of mashed to upset over his head when I rose up, a Napoleon, and said they must separate, which they did – though after ¼ hour we were all having coffee together calm as a pond. I think the cause was not just jam but the subterranean surfacing of stress.

H.H.   22/4/68

Anne sends love and thank you for the words about her mother. Anne said earlier "Now, I am going to answer these obituary letters the DAY they arrive." I think that so far, owing to probates and cupboards, she has answered two . . .

It's no use saying to people PUT NOT THY TRUST IN WILLS. After the death of David Tennant there had been speculation about how much Sabrina [wife of Jonny Gathorne-Hardy] would be left. They are particularly broke and I writhed at their optimism. He was enormously rich, my dear, said Eddie. £50,000 and it may even be £100,000. Anne got a letter this morning from Jonny to say that it will be £3000 at the very most, which will be in trust and totally untouchable. Another 6d a week.

Hon. is gathering his great wings to fly. This morning he has gone into Saxmundham to buy himself a trunk. "You won't mind, my dear, will you, if I fill it with books and things and LEAVE it here until I ask you to have it sent out to Greece." "How do we do that?" "Oh, you just ring up Pickfords in Ipswich. You might just have to tie a ROPE round the trunk." "But if it's full of books, Eddie, nobody will be able to lift it; and how much will it cost?" "About fifty pounds, my dear."

H.H.   9/5/68

. . . It was a GREAT delight to see you so happy in your home. I did LOVE the home, which has the perfect comfort and tranquillity – I think you have been very clever. I loved, too, our walk and our visit to the Trianon and the Chateau. It was the greatest treat – all of it – thank you, thank you. . . .

As I got nearer to Blighty, the damper and colder it became until finally it was an icy drench. The house here is in chaos with the dividing of the chattels and the movers coming on Saturday. This afternoon I got on top of Eddie's wardrobe and found it deep in old razor blades and empty bottles. I had always thought him the only tidy one of our tribe.

In July and August H.H. and Anne were lent a villa in northern Cyprus which belonged to Michael Behrens, Harriet's father-in-law. H.H. wrote, in long-hand, amusing details about the house servants and the visit of their old friend, Frances Partridge.[135] "She has been asked to collect wild flowers for a man who is doing a FLORA of CYPRUS. All the wild flowers are of course utterly dried up in the heat but, evidently, it is of great use having them in pod. So she wrenches up withered old cracklers and puts them in a huge press."

N.M.   6/8/68   Venice

. . . Pompadour has arrived – very pretty – & has thrown me into a fantigne as Rainbird's have included a map of Europe in 1748 which *even I* could see at a glance was all wrong & which, when compared to an historical atlas, is like a Picasso map of a woman, I mean it bears no resemblance whatever. Luckily there will probably be no reviews of an old book, otherwise it will give great joy to somebody, not me . . .

---

135. Frances Partridge (1900–2004), Bloomsbury diarist.

N.M. 24/10/68

. . . I went to sign Le Roi-Soleil at Gallimard's yesterday. Outside somebody had written "a bas les éditions bourgeois," so I told M. Gallimard who said calmly, I expect that's my son.

The postscript to this last letter reads "I love your having a Spy in the Bookshop – I worship his report." This does not survive, but many subsequent reports of mine are quoted in his letters.

H.H. 10/12/68

Senility is descending fast upon me. Before breakfast I went into my writing room and pulled the curtains. After breakfast – just now – I went in again and drew them. It stays dark so long in the mornings now that I suppose I thought the day had already whizzed round into night. . . .

I must go and plant some daffodil bulbs even though it turns me into a rusty croquet hoop, which is infinitely better than Gethsemane[136] in the shop (one's ruin will be worth not being there) . . .

Lucy here last weekend. On the Saturday evening she said a friend was staying near Bungay and was coming for a drink at 9 o'c. At 9.15 friend rang up to say that he had broken down ten miles away, so off I had to go to pick him up out of the dark. There by the verge was what appeared to be a Chinaman of the Tang dynasty – a black moustache which hung down in tails on either side of the mouth, a domed head bald in the centrepiece, a dead white face except for the nose which was bright red from pushing his rotten car through the cold. Lucy said he is very persistent. . . .

---

136. H.H.'s name for the Christmas rush at the bookshop.

1969

In March 1969 N.M. wrote "so pleased to see your lovely mad
typewriting". After thanking him for writing about the death
of Mark Ogilvie Grant ("a body blow"), she admitted that
she had been "flat on my back for a month, sometimes in
agony, always uncomfortable. Much better now but a lump
has been found in the region of my liver & lights – no doubt
THE END." *Thereafter, until her death in 1973, all her letters*
contained details of tests and hideous pain while all H.H.'s
letters conveyed his sadness and sympathy. For the first
few months her handwriting remained firm and she was
determined to continue with her biography of Frederick
the Great. Many of these letters make painful reading: I
have been more drastic than usual in my selections.

H.H.   18/6/69

Because of your horrible torment, I am going to try to give
you an especial shriek from the shop spy dossier.[137] You must
SWEAR not to tell – or else his doom would be unthinkable &
his blood for ever on my hands . . . Poor chap. Anne & I did
damage by going to his wedding (he married a Suffolk girl so
it happened near here). The packer told Mollie we were there
& she said that it was a good thing that she & Handy had not
gone & that she'd always suspected that he (John S.S.) was
"on the wrong side."

---

137. I was now referred to as the shop spy. The quotation from my letter
dealt with Handy's lecture to me on my inadequacies as a bookseller.

N.M. 20/6/69

How I screamed about Handy! Mollie wrote the other day very sweetly really about my illness & then something about the awful way (had I realized?) that you had behaved. I replied I never understood about the Shop Row & never wanted to as I so madly wanted to hunt with the hare & run with the hounds. No reply.

Heywood's next letter (30/6/69) was about Geoffrey Gilmour's visit to Aldeburgh. He was "made a little more uneasy beforehand by Janetta [Jackson][138] & Frances Partridge asking themselves at the same time, but they seemed not to addle one another, & I was able to put her in the room with the bird's nest. English countryside looking its best gave him quite a nostalgia." N.M. and H.H. had a long-standing joke about Geoffrey as a "swinger", so much of the letter was devoted to his account of a "gym display by youths from HMS Ganges." Cynthia Gladwyn [Jebb] had invited the Hills and Gilmour to a luncheon party which was "very enjoyable. Diana Cooper had done something like muddling some pills so was in rather a peculiar condition. She was tart to Robin McDouall. He said, 'How lovely to see you,' She said, 'I've seen too much of you lately.' However, he persisted and things improved." All this made N.M. scream. In her reply she told H.H. about the successor to Marie (her maid) who was called Rasputina because of her curative powers as a masseuse; unfortunately she was also "a hopeless servant & a pathetic study in old-maidery. I'm in a perpetual bad temper, which really is not my nature." She was "working madly" and apologised for the dullness of her letters.

---

138. Janetta Jackson, later Parladé (b. 1922), frequently mentioned in Frances Partridge's diaries.

N.M. 18/9/69

. . . I'm beginning to wish I were dead like practically all my friends but I'd like to finish Frederick first . . . This drunk treatment lasts four days & then we shall see. I wonder why people *like* being drunk – I have always wondered.

H.H. 2/10/69

. . . I wrote to Crafty the other day to say that, if an object which I had left in the shop had not been sold and was not too deeply couched, I would call in to collect it. That had an instantaneous effect – cheque for 15 quid by return. I was told that his excuse for not having done anything sooner was that it was difficult for him as he was "not on speaking terms" with me. That's the first I've heard of the non-speakers. I am baffled and sad as to why the vendetta and smirchings seem to increase rather than fade decently away. Suppose I am Iscariot who has sold them – though they are happier and richer without me. I've thought of writing the libretto if I had more talent, but of course far better that you should from your neutral ground, though I rather feel that you might give it to Puccini rather than B. Britten.

It was reported to me that there were shop volcanics last week while Handy was with the Stanleys[139] in the north. The packer chose that time to disappear, under the influence, for three days. The north was rung 4 times a day and finally Mollie hired a car and was driven down to CATFORD where is the packer home. But that morning the packer had come out of the influence and was on his way to the shop, so only wife and kids were found in Catford – mind you, they got WHAT-FOR all right. . . .

---

139. Michael Stanley and his wife Fortune; when in London, they lived at 39 Charles Street.

Anne and I were sad about Ivy Compton-Burnett.[140] I saw her not long ago. She'd shrunk but still had her darting brain. She died in her home which she'd been frightened of not doing – and she still had a maid. Anne reminded me how Ivy had once said to her about some woman "Well – she had a maid to the end."

N.M.   14/10/69

I'm really better & off to Potsdam[141] on Thursday, taking Woman. Great excitement.

Have you heard that Sergeant[142] went to the bookshop & said to Miss Liz that somebody had told him to consult Miss Forbes. "Who is Miss Forbes?" "It's me." "Oh, I thought you were Mrs Buchanan." Poor Sarge quite astounded by the resulting fireworks.

In his letter of 5/12/69 H.H. wrote mainly about the various books he was reading and recommending to N.M. But he could not resist quoting the latest bulletin in which I had mentioned an engraved invitation to a launch party for Lady Longford's biography of Wellington on which Handy was exceedingly keen: SIR GEORGE & LADY WEIDENFELD AT HOME 9.30pm. addressed to Mr Hayward and Lady Elisabeth Hill. "Far too late for me anyway," Handy said, "as I go to bed then." N.M. addressed her next letter, "My dear Heywood (& Lady Elizabeth)".

---

140. Ivy Compton-Burnett, novelist (1884–1969).
141. To research her book on Frederick the Great.
142. Stuart Preston (b. 1915), art historian.

N.M.   10/12/69

East Germany was a Wow. From the moment we left what Pam calls *Cheque* Point Charlie, Alice in Wonderland set in. I was treated like – not a queen or an empress – but I suppose some kind of superior president. People rose when one entered a room. Curators awaited one on the steps of museums, bowing to the earth. Every queue was jumped. When we entered a restaurant, people were hustled from their table to make way. There were 4 of us, Pam and the Laws; we were never allowed to pay for so much as a cup of coffee & we had two huge Russian cars to take us everywhere. A lord in waiting called Mr Friedlander, never left my side . . .

Of course we saw marvels & the whole journey was indispensable to me for the book. I fell for the beauty of the land, esp. Saxony. But Dresden makes one die of shame. I would much rather live in the East than West Germany, but not for the reasons East Germans would appreciate – viz., as they haven't got round to factory farming, the food tastes heavenly (but, if you say so, they look worried & affirm that next year all the farms will be factories). They have got marvellous roads & you never see another car. The people look poor & sweet – in West Germany they look rich & horrid. But Friedlander assures one that next year the East Germans will be rich & horrid. He rang up a few days ago saying since I've been 10 days with you, I see everything differently. When we parted, he said some Eng. people had told him he would have a ghastly time with me – he said I didn't expect you to be so 'uman. I think he usually takes people to see heavy industry – he'd never had a pen-pusher before & I'm sure never a shrieker. When we arrived at the hotel (23 storeys) at Potsdam, I said, "Pull that down, Mr Friedlander." "But we've only just put it up." "Yes, well, it's a mistake & you'd better pull it down again." An hour later, I got into the lift which then whizzed up & down for 35 minutes without stopping, I thought it was THE END. Pam thought I'd been kidnapped. Apparently it always happens & somebody said I was lucky to have been alone & not with Outer Mongolians, "They *panic*." The only thing that rather spoilt it all was pain, of which I still have a good deal, depending on the day . . .

Imagine how a German wishing to write about George II would be treated in London! By the way, there's a notice in the lift in English: All shakings & violences to the doors & bolts are FORBIDDEN.

1970

. . . There were ten people here for Christmas – Harriet & family & Lucy & Bob [Gathorne-Hardy]. Anne went to bed with 'flu the moment they arrived on Christmas Eve, which was lucky for her though she had it badly and is only just getting better. Harriet was splendid and did all the cooking with no stress or strain and many a shriek. I missed her very much when she left and had to do the nursing and cooking (terrible times with withered goose and clotted packet soup) by myself. Not at all helped by the daily woman who said that Lady Anne ought to sick-up the germ like she had (details were given) . . .

N.M.   22/1/70

Christmas here was such a nightmare that it has passed into legend. I was completely paralysed with my leg – had to go to the bathroom on all fours, no question of stairs. My Belgian *lady* [who had replaced Rasputina] went down with 'flu & said she was only fit to make a little white soup *for herself* – then I got it & so did the femme de ménage . . . Well, I hasten to say it passed over as things do.

On the brighter side, my book has gone to print & Mrs Law came with the smashing pictures she has collected for it & that cheered me up considerably. Now I'm enjoying being able to read other people's efforts. . . .

N.M.   12/2/70

Many thanks for your kind sympathy. Like always with ONE, the sun having come out again, I can hardly remember

Black Christmas or quite see what all the beefing was about. The bright hot sunshine comes mainly from my new servant Hassan (shades of James Elroy [Flecker]) who is a literally first class cook & adorable man; & who, instead of standing over me & boring as the Belgian lady did, does his work & then thinks silently about the desert . . .

I'm adoring *Wellington*[143] – there are such resemblances with F. that it's quite uncanny – esp. the dry jokes & no nonsense. But F.'s battles were *far* more desperate & therefore, exc. for Waterloo, more thrilling. Both men the absolute contrary of the Monty-Nelson school . . .

I've got a letter from Gerry [Wellington] on a cruise saying he finds the middle classes are quite different from *us*, & I ought to write a book about them. Help!

H.H.   4/3/70   Shrubland Hall, Ipswich

I do hope that it's still 3 cheers for Hassan. Such a relief to hear about him . . . I am delighted to have the [Edward] Fitzgerald book. Thank you so much . . . My mother knew the whole of Omar Khayyam by heart (I imagine quite a few mothers did) and my father had hung up, in the downstairs lavatory, the framed farewell signatures of his under officers in the 1st War which began: – TO A GREAT O.C. and had underneath –

> "Turn down an empty glass
> The caravan starts for the dawn of nothing."

I spent hours pondering that and thinking how extraordinary that the 1st World War should be an empty glass and that peace should be the dawn of nothing. I told Edith & Osbert Sitwell about it when they had me over to dinner at

---

143. Elizabeth Longford, *Wellington. Volume I: The Years of the Sword*, 1969.

Renishaw when I was stationed in the stables at Wentworth Woodhouse in the 2nd World War. They were too delicate, I suppose, to tell me that the quotation is from Omar Khayyam, which I only discovered later.

I am in this extraordinary place as [Betty Batten]'s[144] guest . . . I am getting rather hungry as they don't really take "normal" guests – so apart from steam cabinets (those things like steaming hansom cabs), underwater massage and high irrigation, I have to conform and live on raw veg. and slop. Anne tries to make me stuff a pork pie when I visit her,[145] but somehow one doesn't feel like it. . . .

N.M.   8/3/70

. . . I tried to learn O Khayyam by heart at 16 but can't learn anything; I would recognise quotations from it. I still think it very beautiful (!) though now perhaps too Lesley Blanch like. But of course the marvellous perfection of James Elroy [Hassan] is rapidly changing my view of Arabs . . .

My book is being printed. I think it's the best of a poor lot & so do the publishers. However that didn't stop them rewriting it, a fact which faced me ON THE PROOFS. Viz. "a good gossip" became "they reminisced". I made the most fearful fuss & said I would choose freedom – they completely climbed down & now have got to pay huge sums to have my absurdities put back. Do you realise that young Hartington has risen like cream at Rainbird's – they say the ball is at his feet & he is born to direct a large enterprise!

---

144. Betty Batten, close friend and contemporary of H.H.
145. Anne Hill was in an Ipswich nursing home, having a vein operation on both legs.

N.M.   16/3/70

. . . *Come on the* FRANCE. A huge party of friends, headed by [Geoffrey Gilmour] is signing on for "round the world in 80 days" next winter. It's rather exp[ensive] but we think the money must come out of capital; "you can't take it with you" is our motto. As our joint ages add up to several thousands, we realise it's not very likely we shall all come back – not, not the six hundred. Still a funeral or two at sea will pass the time & make a change from St Honoré d'Eglau. Come on. Sell one or two of Eddie's books – tell him I told you so.

H.H.   16/4/70

How I wish that I could come on the FRANCE (I would have brought dozens of union jacks) but our voyage to America (have I dared confess?) [planned to last from June to September] makes it too extravagant. Then in the late autumn I hope we shall go to Italy to stay with Harriet & Tim who have bought a house near Siena to which they migrated at the beginning of the month . . .

I am just beginning Harold [Acton]'s 2nd vol. of autobiog [*More Memoirs of an Aesthete*]. I looked in index to see if you and shop were mentioned and see that the only ref. is that old nut about your turning it into a lit. salon. If only Malcolm was still with us, to tease and remind us of the person who asked "Isn't there some dim little couple in the background?"

Anne gave a tiny strangled shriek when she read the only ref. to her in Jim [Lees-Milne]'s autobiog.[146] Do you remember how he describes that he was extra depressed and says that he had become involved in an "emotional entanglement" and puts a bracket after it saying, "I wanted to get married"?

---

146. James Lees-Milne, *Another Self*, 1970.

Anne mildly told me that they had been engaged for 3 months and that, up to the break, he was v. much in love with her, and that after the break and after she and I had started the shop, he took her out one night and proposed to her again. She is going to write to tell him how the book made her laugh and she is going to sign the letter with love from your emotional entanglement. [Details of the planned trip to America followed.]

N.M.   28/4/70

. . . Oh, Jim & Anne – fancy the old *brute* trying to elope with her – the limit. All my astringent friends are dead: Malcolm, Hinkabelle [Roger Hinks], Robert [Byron], Victor [Cunard], they are the ones I miss. It's a very English attribute – the French don't really tease, I wonder why? Voltaire did but he couldn't take it from others. It must be a two way commerce.

I adored Harold's book. He has hit off Emerald [Cunard] better than anybody: I must say it was hard cheese for her having Daphne [Fielding],[147] who she very much disliked in life, to write about her. Jim's much less good: too farcical & everything wrong (untrue, I mean). . . .

H.H.   14/5/70

I dreamed last night that I met Diana [Mosley] in the Berkeley. It had just been done up (actually it's just been pulled down) and she said to me "I suppose you like this." Then I began to ask her about you and the canned music became louder & louder so that I could not hear what she said and

---

147. Daphne Fielding (1904–97), author of *Emerald and Nancy. Lady Cunard and her Daughter*, 1968.

then we all faded away. She had a wonderful dress on – strawberry coloured. . . .

I felt a twinge of jealousy when I heard that Jim and Alvilde were going to see you. Jim and Anne have been writing one another "emotional entanglement" letters – lovingly reminiscent. . . . I enjoyed Harold's book when I properly read it. Before, I had only done an index reading and hadn't even read all about the shop – about your silver laughter, and me being Hoffmanesque. I liked that . . .

I was endeared by the telephone operator whom Anne got on to yesterday when she was meaning to ask her vein surgeon how much his bill was. She dialled clumsily and thought the operator was the surgeon "Madam, your thoughts are ahead of your numbers" he said – after Anne had asked him how much his bill would be. . . .

N.M.   18/5/70

How awful to think that you will be in that ghastly place [America] until October. Whatever will you DO all day? So dangerous too – it's going down like a ship. Oh, chuck it. And then the garden, how *can* you leave with the roses in bud? . . .

On May 25th, Bank hol. I think, you could hear my ravings on the Home Service at 10.30am (if you were awake). The interviewer, cleverer than most, gave me some good openings . . .

H.H.   26/5/70

Oh MY – it was as if you were in the room. The daily woman "does" the drawing-room Mondays, but I told her that, on this particular one, she'd got to quit by 10.30. ¼ of an hour before, I began tuning in, as of course didn't want to miss a drop. You were preceded by a church service. "I suppose we must all get down on our knees," said the daily.

"You're on them already, Mrs Ling" I answered. After the Blessing Anne & I & Ruth Gathorne-Hardy [wife of Anne Hill's brother Antony], who is staying, settled down to ¾ hour of BLISS. It really was uncanny – the voices – HERE you were – the silver laughter ringing round and Pam's endearingly slow voice. I blubbed when the LOST CHORD began to swell . . .

N.M. 4/10/70

Delighted to have you *sous la main* again – I regard a letter to America as a letter lost & never write any.

A joke I've been saving up to tell you: Pam said "you know that man Handle who works in the bookshop?" Of course I couldn't tell whether it was Handle like the door or Handel like the musician but feel sure it was the former somehow . . .

Frederick comes out tomorrow. I've already had one *awful* review, Plumb in NY Review of Books. I seem to remember his notice of Sun King was even worse – didn't really affect the sales. He calls it Rabbit Pie – what a brute! Why don't these clever people write the books themselves, one wonders? . . .

Grace Dudley[148] has taken me in charge. For two years I've had no new clothes – she forced St Laurent to send down a dress, I can never describe its oddity to the eye of Rip van Winkle; I love it so much, I practically go to bed in it. It's a sack – coloured sack to the ankles, hideous and smart beyond belief. . . .

I shall miss you in London &, once back at home, you'll never want to move again – so we are divorced, I fear.

---

148. Grace Countess of Dudley (b. 1923), née Kolin, married first to Prince Stanislaus Radziwill, then to the 3rd Earl of Dudley.

H.H.   8/10/70   Lecchi-in-Chianti, Siena

Delighted to get your letter, though miserable that you are still in such anguish . . .

I happened to buy a TIMES in Siena with a review of Fred. in it. Immensely grudging. I fear that, now you are on such a summit of popularity, you are bound to be potted at by all the unpopular profs. They are of course listening furiously to the flow of chink. . . .

N.M.   25/10/70   Holland Villas Road, W14

I wonder whether you are back. I'm here with the saintly Loewensteins[149] having treatment which so far has made me considerably worse & I suffer tortures, not in silence either.

I went to see Handle. The old ruffian hadn't got Fred in the window & only one copy in the shop & said there's nothing this autumn exc. *Palmerston* worth reading. I said, "Really Handle" – "Oh, *Frederick* is a picture book." It seems he tells the customers there's nothing about strategy. Never mind – I've pushed Mrs Wilson[150] back in the bestseller list – though even I can't budge Georgette Heyer . . .

A sewer called or said to be called Nancy Milford has written a book.[151] Handle says everybody writes for my two new books – I expect he just sends Milford if you ask me. Why has he got such a down on one? He was very nearly rude, but Miss Liz handed out the champagne welcome.

N.M.   5/11/70   Holland Villas Road, W14

How kind of you to worry about my health. I see at last a ray of daylight . . .

---

149. Prince Rupert Loewenstein (b. 1933), and his wife Josephine.
150. Mary Wilson, *Selected Poems*, 1970.
151. Nancy Milford, *Zelda Fitzgerald: A Biography*, 1970.

I never went back to Handle land – not from pique but because I've been nowhere, just groaning on my bed . . .

H.H. 25/11/70

After Wellington I had to read Carrington[152] – so that I am only today being able to start Fred. The man at the Aldeburgh bookshop lends me books, so I have to read them quickly and cleanly (I mean without honey at breakfast). Of course, I bought Fred but he lent me Carrington (five pounds if you please).

Anne and I went to the private view of Carrington's pictures which was such a pudding of old squashed Bloomsberries as you never saw. Duncan Grant, Frances Partridge, Rosamond Lehmann, Julia [Strachey], Raymond [Mortimer], Penroses[153] . . . Lord Eccles, the new art headmaster,[154] made an unsuitable speech about what a lot of rum people Carrington knew, and how she was only an amateur artist. Rather rot, considering she was at the Slade. We had lent a picture of circus horses which used to hang over the fireplace at Ham Spray. They are great big white horses – almost cart – and it is obviously a village circus but I heard a gent (not a berry) shouting at his woman "Damn fine picture that of the Riding School at Vienna."

The spy had been allowed to represent the shop at the party. He told me that the Bs mean to retire in 3 years time & go to live in Brighton, but Handel will come up to the shop twice a week . . .

I never met Carrington. Did you? I wonder what Diana thought of her. She seems to have caused havoc with her

---

152. *Carrington: Letters and Extracts from her Diaries,* edited by David Garnett, 1970.

153. Roland Penrose and his wife.

154. Viscount Eccles (1904–99), then Minister for the Arts.

lovers – except for Lytton who I suppose was havoc & lover proof – in that direction. I did meet him – several times. In fact remember having a jolly dance with him at the sailor party. . . .

N.M.   5/12/70

You ought not to have bought Fred. I had counted on your borrowing him – such an awful price . . . I long to know what you think of Fred who is by far my favourite – but tell the truth, I shall know if you don't & untruth is so uninteresting. . . .

H.H.   15/12/70

I do deeply grieve that your London expedition only made you worse. I had SO hoped that it would make you better . . .

On the way back [from London] I bought the Evening Standard which I hardly ever see & was immensely rewarded by finding in it Antonia Fraser's excellent review of Fred. It exactly said what I think about it. YOUR BEST. So delightfully readable & full of fascinating interest &, thank goodness, not stuffed with the strategy which Handel so longed for . . .

I hear applause all round. I fear that gov. praise won't count with you but I had a letter this afternoon from my Henry Jamesy spinster about the Christmas presents she was buying for people & she said, "so I chose Nancy Mitford's handsome FREDERICK THE GREAT & looking through it upon coming home was glad I had. It sparkles with intelligence & wit & the coloured plates are absolutely glorious . . . Miss Mitford seems to have gone from strength to strength."

N.M.   20/12/70

How one loves praise. Specially unqualified! Thank you very much for all you say. Of course it all comes (the success, if it exists) from the marvellous subject – I shall never find another like that. Antonia's review was a nice Christmas box after what I call the Lady Writer Putter Righters & their ineffable spite. The best constructive review was in The Times, it was perfectly fair, well informed & pretty favourable. What I object to is the reviewer who hasn't bothered to mug up the subject & who says things like "Miss M. asks us to believe that Frederick was a brilliant writer – I wonder!" . . .

1971

Just listen to this. My neighbour, who is also my guardian angel on whom I *utterly depend*, Mme Suchard, asked if I could suggest some light English books for her to give her nephew & GODson of 17, a lazy boy who is learning English. So I explained to Miss Liz & asked for £5 worth of Penguins & such like. The parcel arrived & I sent it straight over to Mme S. The next day she loomed, saying, "these books – you know we are not very go-ahead in my family – could you very kindly see if they are really suitable for a young boy?" Well, two of them had disgusting naked women on the covers. I got away with them (as they were called things like *Rose of Tibet*) by saying the women were goddesses. The third had a picture of a boy dressed for cricket fondling a naked lady (my dear, lucky it *was* a lady, in view of the contents) & written on the cover "A novel of strange vices" which of course even Mme Suchard could translate. I simply grovelled – said I couldn't believe it of MY MOTHER's old bookshop, one of the most respectable in London. (Didn't mention Handy's activities in the basement.) But Mme S. will never view me with the same eye again – the worst was that Nicole the daughter undid the parcel & said "O là, Maman, tu fais des progrès"! Mme S was furious to be caught out making such progress. Honestly how could Miss Liz have done such a thing?

Well, I couldn't be bothered to send back strange vices & I read it – *too* brilliant, screamingly funny & disgusting beyond belief. It's calling *Fielding Gray* by S[imon] Raven – I do recommend it.

H.H. 17/1/71

. . . Of course I shrieked over Mme Suchard's progress. Just shows what the permissive society has done to Curzon Street (or maybe it's the other way round) . . .

While searching for something for [Ralph Jarvis[155]] to read, I came across a little pamphlet called CORNISHIANA which consists of the collected sayings of a woman called Mrs Warre-Cornish who was the wife of the Provost (I think) of Eton. I wonder if you ever saw it. "Tell me," said Mrs Cornish to a young lady, "whom would you rather have for a lover – Shelley, Keats or Byron?" The young lady being too shy to speak, Mrs Cornish answered her own question "I'd give all three of them for one wild half hour with Rossetti." . . . Would you like me to send it you? . . .

I fear my quotation from Cornishiana will seem weak as water to you after the startling "progress" which you have been making with STRANGE VICES . . .

During her "horrid treatment" for the next few months, N.M. did not write. H.H. heard news of her illness from various London friends and sent several letters: about the death of one of his oldest and closest friends, Betty Batten; about the birth of his daughter Lucy's son in Delhi; and about Harriet and Tim Behrens's life in Tuscany. On 23 March he wrote: "Not much to tell you from here – except about DRAINS. They have all gone wrong & I am in despair. A bulldozer has been dozing a large part of the garden and making it look like World War One because THEY told me that there must be a new SOAKAWAY (hideous word and thought). They have dozed up some of my most

---

155. One of Anne's cousins, and an old Cambridge friend of Heywood.

precious shrubs – as well as the whole thing being total ruin.
. . . Anne had one of her IDEAS. She told the bulldozers to
build an artificial mountain with the earth they had dozed.
The result is the most queer-looking mound. We have
discovered that it's full of glass from Eddie's old gin bottles,
so that won't be very good for the kids when they make their
scenic slides (part of Anne's plan), though she says they
won't feel the glass so much when the mound is covered
with grass."

H.H. 17/4/71

. . . Eddie hasn't written for months but I did hear fairly
lately that he had been staying with the Leigh Fermors and
that Joan had said that she likes having him because he is so
selfish that there is no doubt what he wants. A point of view, I
suppose, though charitable.

One of Anne's other brothers Bob – the one who talks hind
legs off people – has been staying with Harriet. H. writes "At
the end of one long talkative evening, I had gone to bed. I
heard Bob saying to Tim, Well, my dear, I must say I think
Gray's Elegy is one of the really GREAT works of art (humm,
sniff, snort). Well, I think, replied Tim, it's the biggest load of
crap I've ever read. Bob got up & went to bed."

N.M. 11/5/71

Perhaps I owe you a letter. I am very ill – haven't left my
room for three weeks, & in tortures or else poisoned by these
hateful drugs. . . .

I loved those books you recommended. I can easily get
through a book a day & am frantic when without one. I've
sent to Handle for a mass of Penguin classics & meanwhile
I'm in [Mapp &] Lucia but I know her too much by heart.
Somebody gave me *First Circle*; you may imagine I had to be

desperate to read it but, once begun, I was entranced. Can I face *Cancer Ward*?[156] A bit too near home, I think . . .

H.H.   15/5/71

. . . You ask about the Moslems [Lucy and her Scottish husband Geordie had converted to Islam]. They have been here for 3 weeks . . . Moslemism isn't evident. I mean that Anne doesn't have to shout from the minaret, though I have seen some beads (I presume a Moslem rosary) hung on the end of the bed. I rather think that the birth of a baby – combined with the horrors of India – weakened religious fervour. They asked a friend down last week whom I did not adore.[157] He had been the husband of Marianne Faithfull who was snatched from him by Mick Jagger of the Rolling Stones. He had matted hair going grey half way down his back, torn jeans and a dirty shirt which had more holes than shirt, and gold-rimmed spectacles. I went into his room when he was out to see if it was all right & opened an ms. notebook which he'd left on a table. The first thing I read was CORRUPTION IS THE INSURANCE AGAINST UNCERTAINTY. I don't know what that means but it made me uneasy. . . .

[Next week] Anne & I are going to stay with the Vyners in Sussex; they are NOT hell [as Nancy had been told in a letter from Mollie]. Margaret is so terrified by Liz and Mollie that she never dares to go near the shop. Henry is lazy but I should have thought that would suit Handy because he can do most of his Handling undisturbed.

---

156. By Alexander Solzhenitsyn: *First Circle*, 1968; *Cancer Ward*, Part 1 1968, Part 2 1969.
157. John Dunbar.

H.H   2/6/71

I cannot remember if I wrote to you during our damp round of visits. I believe I began & never ended. On the way to the Vyners our behind was run into by a horrid little man suitably called Mr Buttivant. . . . We were able to go on in spite of a buckled bumper and a crumpled boot. Utterly maddening as it was a new car which we were running in.

There was a man called Arthur Marshall[158] also staying with the Vyners. He's the one who imitates hospital matrons on the wireless. Rather like a jolly matron himself and v. much in the Binkie [Beaumont][159] world. . . .

After that we went on to Bob near Newbury. He took us one day to see his & Anne's cousin, Geoffrey Gathorne-Hardy, who is 93, and his wife, who is 95. He has got a quite staggering collection of Old Master drawings. We were taken to the billiard room where some were hanging. All the mouldering curtains were drawn against the sun (it was raining) & cousin Geoffrey started tugging at their pulleys, but they didn't budge an inch. Then cousin Kathleen began to tug but with no more result, and cousin G. started shouting DON'T KATHLEEN, GO AWAY. She was enjoying herself & wouldn't go away except to fetch a candle. Then Bob took us upstairs to a peeling bedroom where the best of the drawings were kept in a cupboard for "safety" – two Leonardos, two Rembrandts, a Durer, a Carpaccio & many others. Terrifying to think of the burgle possibilities. I fear that, although they have no children, there is not one ray of hope that Anne could inherit, though Bob is thought to have a chance. (Actually, they would probably be a liability – too dangerous to hang & look at in the home & probably not allowed to be sold).

---

158. Arthur Marshall (1910–89), author and television personality.
159. H. G. Beaumont (1908–73), distinguished theatre manager.

Then on to the Lees-Milnes. That was particularly enjoyable – it all looked so pretty – the crammed garden all bursting out – so lush (making one green after sandy Snape) and
themselves seemingly far more harmonious. We went to
dinner with Caroline Somerset & her husband[160] in their
pretty house on the edge of Badminton. Belonging to the jet
set, as Alvilde described them, so Anne & I were frightened,
but their manners were too good to allow one to be sprinkled.
Then another day there was one of those Westminster
Duchesses: Sally, the widow of the Duke before this . . .
Alvilde did no mincing of matter over her scorn of the garden
which was a vast length of lawn with random placing of beds.
She (the duchess) told me how she had bought some v. expensive old book from the shop. "I was told", she said, "that I
could return it whenever I wanted to – so one day I thought I
would, but the extraordinary thing is that, though I wrote to
that nice little man there, I could get no answer to my letters."
However, she did very well because she sold it to Maggs in the
end for double what she had paid for it.

N.M.   5/6/71

Oh the brute (yr. motor), what misery. That's the reason
why I will not own a car – too much trouble. I love the
account of your tour esp. the Old Masters. Oh I say! It's so
nice looking at them quietly, isn't it – I know from Chatsworth. Drawings ought to be owned by *people*, not museums.
. . . I love the Somersets &, if younger, would be IN love with
him . . .

The BBC (télé) are going to do a Mitford Saga in 14 episodes from my books. What a lark. But it will probably take
four years so we shall all be dead.

---

160. David Somerset (b. 1928), who succeeded his uncle as Duke of
Beaufort.

I've read *Dinner at Magny's*[161] and *Verlaine*,[162] both confirming me in my loathing for the 19th cent. V. a bit near the knuckle for anybody who has lived with a drunk.[163] . . .

H.H. 18/6/71

. . . The [Aldeburgh] Festival is some days rather a nightmare what with all the "lovely" people that descend. Yesterday there were some extra lovely ones planted upon us by a blind man who had stayed with Sheila last year. The blind man's name is Roger Butler but Anne wrote to the people who were staying in Aldeburgh, to say that she had heard from Roger BANNISTER about them & would they come over – so there was some confusion . . .

The Queen Mother came to a concert last Sunday & had lunch with the Penns.[164] Fidelity [Cranbrook] who was there too, told me that she (the Q.M.) had two dry martinis before, wine during, and two glasses of port after, and that everyone was exhausted by trying to keep up with the consumption. Fidelity is no consumer herself, however, and is famous for her thimbles of Cyprus sherry. The Q.M. buys 250 hams a year from a grocer in Peasenhall which is a village near here. I'm told she takes a ham sandwich to bed every night – no matter how big the banquet . . .

N.M. 22/6/71

. . . Debo's tales of the Q. Mother would make a lovely book (a Rainbird book). The other day, temp 50°, clad in

---

161. Robert Baldick, *Dinner at Magny's*, 1971.

162. Harold Nicolson, *Paul Verlaine*, 1921.

163. A reference to her ex-husband, Peter Rodd.

164. Sir Eric and Lady Penn, who lived at Sternfield House near Saxmundham.

sleeveless satin, she sat next the communist Mayor of Derby – wooed him, won him; asked for a *teeny* cutting of the geraniums with which the room was decorated. Later, Debo saw about 40 huge pots being loaded into the Royal Boot – the wrong sort of geranium.

N.M.   11/7/71

. . . The bookshop, to do it justice, (miss Liz, I guess) has saved my life by sending me a lot of proofs of new books. How badly people do write nowadays. There's a book on the Hohenzollerns which I fell upon;[165] it seems to be written by an Indian, full of old fashioned slang & mixed metaphors. The part about Fred copied from mine in another idiom. He is finally described as a bitchy queen. Ha ha. I look forward to James P[ope]-H[ennessy]'s life of Trollope. I've just read *The Duke's Children* & marvelled again at T.'s understanding of the very grand. How did he do it? . . .

A man has adapted Pomp. as a wireless play – he says twice "they told the king & I" – gross historical mistakes abound, & people address the King as Louis! I've begged that my name should be left out, but will it be? I never saw such an effort – how can such people be employed by the BBC?

H.H.   20/7/71

. . . Cynthia rang me up on Sunday morning at 10 to 11 & was beginning to tell me how you couldn't get to a faith healer, but I had to stop her as we were actually taking Frances & Algy, the grandchildren, to church which began at 11. I am an old sceptic [about faith healing] and haven't much faith, but one never QUITE knows and you must desperately

---

165. W. H. Nelson, *The Soldier Kings: The House of Hohenzollern*, 1971.

feel that you will try ANYTHING. I suppose that those were Anne's feelings about church, but we'd forgotten quite how long & boring it can be. . . . The only thing which riveted the children was the first lesson which was about Jael driving a nail into Sisera's head. Our fear is that it may have given Algy ideas – though today Anne & I are like clumsy Jaels ourselves as we are trying and utterly failing to pitch the tent which Fanny was given yesterday for her birthday . . .

I have to write to you improperly – between the scamperings of little feet. The result of taking them to church has been a battery of questions about the deity. Fanny has said that Kate – her ½ sister – told her that God is an animal . . .

N.M.   2/8/71

. . . Faithful Joy Law arrived with 20 books she had wormed out of various publishers, so I'm all right for a bit, though I plainly see I shall only be able to read ¼ of them – viz. there are two by L. P. Hartley! I'm enjoying one proof about Chelsea by a lady writer called Holme. I suppose it will eventually be Rainbird & ought to be very pretty.[166] My nephews who work there (& simply adore it) say that there are two hats, one full of subjects & the other of authors. I suppose that is why we got [J. B.] Priestley on the Regent, what Joy calls a non-book if ever there was one. What do you feel about illustrated books? Now that I am used to them, I feel the need for pictures & really hate reading (as in a new life of Rudolf II) about agate vases which I can't see. Also I do love to know what people looked like. I think the ideal is my Pomp: in pocket sized well printed paper back.

---

166. Thea Holme, *Chelsea*, 1972.

N.M.   21/8/71

. . . That old Tartuffe Handy hasn't got any of my books in stock. Diana dashed in to get some to give away – blank. Being faithful her, she took a cab to Truslove & found all. But you & I know another customer would have taken something else. It's very grave for me because I can't write & depend on old books. Isn't he an old brute?

Colonel produced the Comte de Monte Cristo & I've lived in it for 4 days – it's immensely long & am now utterly bereft. You can't imagine the fascination & I'm sure you'll never try it. I wouldn't have exc: that I was down to zero in the book line . . .

If I can ever revive (but I seem to get worse), I'll write memoires beginning 1945 – like that I won't re-bore people with Uncle Matthew & all the stuff in my novels & I'll have something I can write without research. My memory is poor but selective, & I dare say I won't tell more lies than most people do.

Letters to England have gone up to 2/-, isn't it vile? But if you join the C[ommon] M[arket], they will be half that.

H.H.   17/9/71

I had a disturbing dream about you last night. I was in some flat in Bayswater where I had never been, when you came & visited. I can't remember about the visit or what you said which was so funny about the saddle of a bicycle – but I do remember that I was very worried that you had to go down so many stairs. I rang up a taxi for you, but of course it did not arrive and you began to walk down the street. I was walking ahead of you wildly shrieking for taxis, when I looked round, you had disappeared. I found you sitting in one of those awful submerged areas of Victorian Bayswater houses. You said you could go no further. Not a jolly dream, but I tell you to prove how I do fret about you.

We have been away for nearly a fortnight . . . we ended up with [Lees & Mary] Mayall at Sturford Mead.[167] Lees told us some funny stories about his diplomatic life. He told how Henry Bath[168] had gone up to some Japanese high-up embassy person – a woman – and said "Do you have FOOD in your country?" Also, how he (Lees) had to introduce some Eastern ambassador called U CHIT to the Queen – so he had to shout out U CHIT, MA'AM (the C should be pronounced S but Lees decently cheated).

H.H. 1/10/71

After she had read your last letter, Anne said "I think Nancy must be a saint." I said "Why? Do you mean because of her hideous endurance test and the way she has endured it?" "No," Anne answered, "I mean because of the way she treats servants. Do you remember how good she was to that ghastly old Norway?[169] How she used to take her bottles of brandy in the middle of the war?"

Talking of servants, I was reading Emily Eden's *Semi-Attached Couple* in bed last night. Mrs Douglas says "I am always glad of an opportunity to tell servants what a thoroughly bad race they are." Of course, that was written in the 1830s – a most enjoyable snobbish book . . . Anne claims that it was she who first invented the word "gov" – when one day she said to you in the shop how all Yanks are like governesses. Do you remember?

I met Eddie at Saxmundham station last night. He tottered out of a first class with an ivory-handled Byronic stick and a golfer's gamp and a small grip of appalling weight (bottles

---

167. Lees Mayall (1915–92), head of Protocol and later Ambassador to Venezuela, had been H.H.'s best customer for new books over several years.
168. Lord Bath, father of the present Marquess, owner of Longleat.
169. See note 21.

and books). CAN YOU CARRY THIS MY DEAR? were his
first words. How are you? I asked. AGED and IMPOTENT,
my dear.

N.M. 14/10/71

Servants – I am going to deal with them in my memoirs. Of
course I have been lucky: Marie, had she had schooling would
have been an intellectual; Sigrid to whom I still write & who
came to see me in London, the same; Gladys was a noble
peasant & Hassan is a noble savage. Did I tell you that he
writes *votre fidèle serviteur*? Well, this morning he returned.
He had bought me a present, a vase 3 feet high, blue & red &
gold glass. All I can say my guardian angel was on the boat. A
young tourist smashed it with her valise. Oh, it's too agonis-
ing and ecstatic. Imagine what it must have cost. I said, But
what did you do? He took the valise and threw it in the sea. A
porter had to dive after it & Beamish [Hassan] was arrested.
But I gather that when the police heard his tale, they all began
to cry in unison & Beamish got off.

I think the relationship of people with their servants was
perfect in the 18th cent.. I believe the secret is to make them
feel the whole show belongs to them. I always say we: we've
got so & so for dinner. *Our* garden is looking too lovely –
when I don't say *your*.

H.H. 25/10/71

The Lees Mayalls came for the weekend a fortnight ago.
They & Eddie & I went to have a drink with John & Sheila
[Hill] on Saturday evening. Anne stayed behind to cook.
When we got back, Anne said that dinner wasn't ready so
they had more to drink and became hilarious, to put it mild.
As usual, it was the good and prim who suffered. Anne was
getting the dinner when her rope soles slipped on the tiled

floor of the hall. I was telephoning in the drawing room & I heard her shout I AM HURT. I dashed out and was appalled to see her lying there immobile and with blood all over her face. She had knocked her forehead while falling but it was really her leg she had hurt. [It had been fractured] . . . The drink had made the Mayalls & Eddie rather over-solicitous & to revolve – wanting to do things & not knowing what. There was a paralysing moment when Anne asked Eddie what her wound looked like & he answered "It looks, my dear, like the c—t of a Maltese goat."

Anne is still in a nursing home in Ipswich. Hardly any pain & I think really enjoying herself. She is helping [William St. Clair] to edit a new edition of Trelawny's *Adventures of a Younger Son*[170] – so this is a splendid opportunity for her to be able to do the research which the cook-housekeeper life here makes difficult for her. The not so enjoyable time will be when she is expelled from the nursing home on crutches . . .

N.M. 2/11/71

I don't think I ever said how sorry I am about "I am hurt". Is Anne all right now?

Now I realize there's nothing much to tell. Diana, my link with the outside, is away & Gaston is only a link with people unknown to you. Beamish (Hassan) is too good to be really funny – thank heaven because, ill as I am, it would be upsetting to have somebody on whom one could not rely. . . .

Money is nothing to him. He gave me a present costing, I am told, about £50 in the form of a Moroccan pouf of rare hideosity. He said to Mme G. [the daily], I can't bear to see her sitting on the floor. To the horror of Geoffrey I have installed it in a place of honour, saying people mean more than things.

---

170. Edward Trelawny, *Adventures of a Younger Son*, edited with an introduction by William St. Clair, 1974.

H.H.   15/11/71

I think you like being kept up-to-date with the history of the shop – so I have made a copy of a letter from Henry Vyner which arrived last week.[171]

I tremble to think what quakes must be happening in Curzon Street. I have never been forgiven for escaping from being "undermined" – even though I gave the old sapper a year's notice – , so what can be the result of no notice at all?

H.H.   21–28/12/71

Being head housemaid here doesn't leave me much time, you can be sure of that, to wish you a white Christmas, but I'm going to try all the same.

I was in Oxford Circus tube station only last week changing on to the Bakerloo when I saw a girl wandering down the platform in a skirt to the ground reading a book. I longed to know what the book was so, in danger of being a filthy old man, I crept up and looked over her shoulder. It was THE SUN KING in paperback . . .

I began this letter 4 days before Christmas but now it is three days after. Christmas crashed down like a great iron curtain &, what with Anne being on crutches & the young being Muslims and trusting in Allah to provide, there was a lot to be done. Especially as 20 relations came to a party & I had to dress up in Ruth Gathorne-Hardy's red nightdress & a Father Christmas beard & appear from behind the trees with the headlights of the car shining upon me. The heavy sack nearly made me fall backwards into the rock garden.

---

171. This told H.H. that he had sold the bookshop, at a considerable profit to himself, to David Bacon, a customer whose offices were close by in Queen Street.

1972

From the beginning of 1972 N.M.'s handwriting deteriorated. On 2 January she could feel "the dottiness coming over me – I'll finish tomorrow" and, when her hand was firmer, wrote that, if she had continued this letter, it would have been full of meat for the psychoanalyst. On the same day H.H. was describing the problems of the Muslim names now taken by Lucy and her family and their insistence on food that was home-made, compost-grown and vegetarian.

H.H.   17/1/72

About your bookworm niece [who wanted to know the name of a reliable English bookshop], I don't think the Aldeburgh shop. To my deep dismay, the wonderful present owner is retiring in September (Anne says that it's my fault, because his wife has seen how much I'm enjoying being retired & is making him do the same).

I'm sure that Liz or John S.S. at Curzon Street, if they knew it was through you (if they thought it was me, she'd be instantly excommunicated), would take trouble. Otherwise there's John Sandoe,[172] who has reputation of being immensely efficient and good.

John S.S. came & had lunch here after Christmas while he was staying with his in-laws in Dedham which is not far away. He told me that Bacon [the new owner] is being adroit . . . he had been for a drink in Earls Court and had been shown a ledger & he'd said that it was the finest bit of accountswomanship that he'd ever seen – since which there hasn't been so much as a whisper.

---

172. Bookshop off King's Road, Chelsea.

One day he [John] had gone out early to lunch from the shop when his brother came in & asked where he was. "We don't know and we couldn't care less," a voice shouted from the inner sanctum.

N.M.   13/2/72

. . . Alvilde came for a night, so good of her. But oh how depressing she is, absolutely nothing is right. Except me. She is one of those who don't notice if you've got a pain & she kept saying how splendid I am. In fact, I'm at the end of my tether, in black despair. . . .

H.H.   15/2/72

As you well know by now all too well (through being bored by blackout stories like one used to be bored by bomb stories), we are all here tripping quaintly about with rushlight and taper. EVERYthing in this house – heating, cooking, water & sewage – is controlled by electricity so that we shall be in a pickle if this strike continues[173] . . . Anne & I went & bought a dreadful little oil cooker. When Anne tried to fill the little rotter, it caused a paraffin flood all over the kitchen floor. She can now lurch without a stick – one can't call it walking – but by taking tiny upright mincing steps we hope to eliminate the limp, though, as you will imagine, Anne is no mincer.

[After seeing Noël Coward's *Brief Encounter* on television] Anne said SHE didn't remember people behaving like that in the thirties and she told me a story which she had never told me before. One day, when she was walking out with Jim L-M, they went back to the flat in King's Bench Walk which he was sharing with Patrick Kinross. They opened the front door & Patrick's voice shouted from some inner room "Vous ne

---

173. The strike caused power shortages that led to a three-day week.

pouvez pas entrer; il y a une femme ici qui vient d'être eu." So they had to leave.

H.H.   17/3/72

Crossing of our last letters. I would have written before, but it has taken a long time to help bury an old aunt (my mother's sister). First of all, Anne & I had to go & spend a night in her house with her son so as to go to the cremation the next day near loathsome Luton. The house had been burned down in the 1st war and my uncle had built it up again into the completest beamy fake I've ever seen – scouring the country for old panels and latchets. The best bedroom, into which Anne & I were put, has old lattice windows which were somehow filched from Jesus College, Cambridge. They do not fit. So the wind howls through them & Anne & I lay in bed with our few hairs blowing as if out-of-doors. There is no running water in the bedrooms. China jugs and basins and slop-pails. A can of hot water was brought up in the morning, which I thought would never happen to me again. The aunt had been an ardent modern-world-hater and refused to relinquish her old standards and kept maids & grooms & horses to the end, and brilliantly managed to make her money just last. Another few months & there would have been less than nothing. . . .

Anne's brother Bob has really had his hope fulfilled. His cousin Geoffrey Gathorne-Hardy, who died a month or two ago, aged over 90, left him [his] collection of Old Master drawings. But the legacy is letting loose a hornet's nest upon him. He was left no money with the drawings . . . Anne is, as usual, having to be a buffer and is getting lots of buffs & no benefits . . .

[We] are going to Italy on April 6 & will be away about a month.

N.M.'s next letter (27/3/72) was written on old Heywood Hill
writing paper, the design of which did not change for 40
years. It was devoted to problems of the Portuguese woman
who looked after her on Sundays and had just thrown her
hand in. Her sister Pam Jackson had solved this but "then
burst out about the extreme filth of my house." She admitted
to having been spoilt by Marie who was "a cleaning maniac".
She had just read Hayter of the Bourgeoisie *by Teresa Hayter,*
daughter of her old friend Sir William Hayter:[174] *"it makes*
my blood run cold."

N.M.   1/6/72

Thanks for lovely letter. I am miles better . . . I've had
exactly 3½ years but many victims have it for life. . . .

I'm getting, or so I suppose, the C.B.E. Apparently it is a
dread secret until announced by the Queen. WHEN? So keep
it under your hat. Assuming that these things are meant for a
spot of boasting, I told one or two loved ones & Diana
Coo[per] was sitting with me when the Intimation arrived
from the Embassy. I was rather pleased, I must confess. Then
a p.c. from Robin McD[ouall] saying if I went on being so
indiscreet it would be *withdrawn*, upon which I was seized
with a wild desire for it & lips, a bit late, were sealed. . . .

N.M.   26/6/72

Oh good – a letter to enjoy. My regulars seem to be holding
off & the old friends only congratulating are generally dull.
(In Eddy Sackville-[West]'s voice please): Oh NO NOT on an
envelope. Really because it [C.B.E.] is so shamingly mere, but
in truth because one is a Hon. & as we still live in a hereditary

---

174. Sir William Hayter (1906–95), diplomat and Warden of New College,
Oxford; brother of the writer Alethea Hayter.

regime, that beats the lot, even V.C.!! . . . I hear that a very short time ago [Cyril] was saying that he would not accept anything under C.H. – how very unwise!

H.H.   26/9/72

. . . It was quite a shock moving on [from the Vyners] to Anne's brother [Bob] in his damp mill house: festoons of cobwebs, birds mess on the pane & pillows like the block. He is so short-sighted that he cannot see the grass & is anyhow utterly impervious to comfort. A good cook, however, & so kind at bottom that one cannot help melting (Anne's older brother, Jock, came to lunch here yesterday & said to Anne "Of course, Bob & Antony & you are all mad. Eddie and I are the only sane ones in the family." I'm not so sure. From being a specialist on Bats he has now moved on to Snails). Rotting old books tumble out of cupboards when you open them. Anne & I tremble for the safety of the Old Master drawings which he has inherited & which he is going to keep in his bedroom & have it wired to the police station.

In early October N.M. went into the Nuffield Nursing Home, Bryanston Square; she had tried English doctors before, but this was her first stay in a London hospital. H.H. sent a small collection of old books he'd chosen for her to read. This included Emily Eden's Letters from India. *"It was published 100 years ago," he wrote "and this copy looks as if it had been couched in a bath for most of that time. I suspect that it is really only the result of Gathorne-Hardy treatment."*

N.M.   15/10/72   Nuffield

Nothing could give me more pleasure than the Couched in the Bath books – they provide the calm yet interesting reading that I need – no shocks like Lord George Curzon – I suppose the new school speaks of Lord George Byron & Lady Lizzie Eustace.

All the same there are some good new books of which *Nancy* is one,[175] a tour de force because one loathes her on every page & yet one reads!

Your books were nearly couched in marmalade too. ALL crashed to earth under a tray, I couldn't look. But when the nurse came, the marmalade jar had held firm. I never would have believed it. . . .

I often think how Mrs Hammersley would have loved my misfortunes & lapped them up – whereas Debo & the others can hardly bear them. If only pain killers would kill pain.[176]

H.H.   26/10/72

Pam Schreiber [a friend who lived near Biddesden, Hants] took us to lunch with Marjorie Brecknock (a whole grouse each) who has been head of every womans' military service & stands in front of the fire, legs astride & hands deep in trousers. She is 72. She had had an interesting burglary. One night a few months ago, two men had got through the drawing room window although it has a shutter with an iron bar across it. The floor was wired to the police station & they managed to step over the wires but they forgot about the ray when making for a glass-topped table full of snuff-boxes. So the alarm went off in the police station & in Marjorie's room – she locked the door & stayed there as she had been told to do. The men were out on the lawn stuffing objects into slit cushions when they saw the headlights of the police car. They bolted in separate cars in different directions. The younger one was a new boy & drove too fast so that a police patrol car was suspicious & chased him & eventually rammed him. He

---

175. Christopher Sykes, *Nancy: The Life of Lady Astor*, 1972.
176. She had eventually been diagnosed as having cancer.

thought he had left all the loot behind, but a small key of a clock was found in his pocket which convicted him. The police questioned him about the other man & he let out that his Christian name was Jerry. So they went to the expensive Kensington flat where they knew of a likely Jerry (57 & a bachelor with 38 suits), & on him they found a tiny valueless owl which Pam had once given Marjorie. He had burgled all his life & got 6 years.

The odd thing was that he wrote from prison a charming letter to Marjorie saying that he did hope she hadn't been too frightened & that, if she had come downstairs, he promises that he would not have mugged her. He finished up "Yours truly or sincerely would not come well from me, so I sign myself yours humbly." What insulted Marjorie was that the police discovered that they had really meant to burgle Hackwood[177] but found they could not get there in time so chose her instead.

N.M.   28/10/72   Nuffield

. . . I so much loved Emily Eden – you were good to pluck it from your breast. Now I'm *living* in Wellington[178] with an interlude of Muggeridge[179] – oh, the cleverness, the jokes & the squalor, I'm so glad to have finished it but would not have missed. I can't say he is my hero but the book saw me through some simply awful nights. I like to think *one's* books sometimes do that for people – if so, it makes up for all the grinding hard work.

Quite ruined money-wise – am trying to think what I can sell & find I love my things so that anything will be a wrench.

---

177. Home of Lord Camrose, near Basingstoke.
178. Elizabeth Longford, *Wellington. Volume II: Pillar of State*, 1972.
179. Malcolm Muggeridge, *Chronicles of Wasted Time. Volume I: The Green Stick*, 1972.

H.H.   10/11/72

. . . How awful for you having to think about selling beloved objets. I have thought of you lying there, listening to that dread tick of the money metre. One hears that tick quite loud enough in one's walking life anyway and, having also that same love of objets, I do feel a true compassion.

N.M.   23/11/72   Nuffield

Those flowers are the prettiest I've had for an age, oh thank you, & also for the Eye.[180] I expect you realise, from my never writing, that I've been excessively ill, such horrid pain.

H.H.   5/12/72

. . . Anne has been making some notes about the early history of the shop. I am appalled to see what a wretched wage you were paid. £3 a week. I had £6. When the clever old artful dodger arrived three years later, he jolly soon was getting £27. But I believe that, if it had not been for that early stingery, the shop would never have survived – founded as it was on a pittance . . .

N.M.   29/12/72   Nuffield

At last at last I feel capable of writing a letter. I do hope you realised that I *couldn't* – a great deprivation as you know how much I enjoy my correspondence, especially that with you. . . .

I've got various books of yours. It would be too wonderful if you had to come up for some purpose & would combine it with picking them up & having a chat. I can even offer a modest viz. revolting luncheon – at 12 noon.

---

180. An issue of the satirical magazine *Private Eye*.

1973

It was so unlucky that I happened to be so bad the day you came – quite unusual. Oh *do* come again. Also we forgot the books you lent me – but don't worry about them, the worst that could happen they'd be left to call for at Chesterfield St.[181]

H.H.   15/1/73

It was a delight to see you standing there and looking so elegant and handsome. I do pray that one was not too exhausting for you – also that I did not do too much JUMPING. I was flattered when you said that you allow hardly any men to see you, though was made a little uneasy when you added that it's because men jump about so . . .

N.M.   28/1/73   Nuffield

I worry about your books . . . What a bore you all are to have quarrelled with the dear old bookshop: makes life insupportable for your friends . . .

In an unusually undated letter N.M. adds, "What a pity there is no longer a central bookshop where they know who has got what. I've got 3 Nancys, 2 Muggeridges, 2 Q. Victorias & don't see how one [exchanges?]. I can't."

---

181. The London home of the Duke of Devonshire.

H.H.   24/2/73

I have been fickle of late for which I do beg pardon but various thwarting things have been happening. The worst was the death of Anne's brother Bob. He was the least expected to die as always seemed unquenchably dynamic but he had to have a small operation on his hand & the anaesthetic gave him jaundice (million to one chance) & he had a v.bad liver from lots of drink & that did quench him. . . . He was a great non-thrower and Anne is going to have to spend about 3 weeks in his house clearing and sorting. V. difficult as there must be a good many lit. relics (all the Logan Pearsall Smith stuff, etc) . . .

I gather that great boilings have been going on in the shop. The new owner has got a new woman instead of Mollie . . . and Liz is said to be leaving. All this may be just gossip – so don't breathe too many words.

N.M.'s next letter, 2 March, came from Versailles, and was addressed to Anne, condoling on the death of her brother. She was more than usually depressed about doctors and her never-ending pain.

H.H.   29/3/73   Tuscany

. . . How relieving that you are RICH. I've been fretting about how you MUST be in a serious dwindle because of enormous doctor & hospital bills.

In a long hand-written letter H.H. reported on volcanic happenings in Curzon Street. David Bacon had indeed asked Mollie to leave. He expected that Handy, who was then on holiday, would also resign but I assured him that this would not happen. I had passed on some of the protagonists'

remarks "in a rather incoherent letter, whose writer was
obviously still suffering from blast." H.H. *was pleased that he*
had been demoted from his position as Enemy No. 1.

N.M.   2/4/73

. . . The Twilight of the Shop is rather dread, isn't it? One
still gets those incredible parcels sent by kind friends – glossy
horrors: Handy says you would like this. I would *not*. I am
loving [Gibbon's] *Decline and Fall* more & more – it's so nice
& long – like eating real cheese.

I wonder why everybody dies except me – fancy Noel
[Coward] & Binkie [Beaumont] on almost the same day.

H.H.   9/4/73

I dreamed last night that I was going to see you but that
your directions about where you now live were a bit vague.
You said that it was near St James's Park Underground station
in a house that had belonged to Rossetti. I came up from that
underground and had quite a time looking for a house with a
plaque on it. Then I went to a Club and began to search in a
Dict. of Nat. Biog. which is the last I remember . . .

I don't believe that the shop crisis means that the shop will
collapse. I'm sure Handy will now go on working there till he
drops. Also, John S.S. is very efficient and nice; Anne got him
down to buy some of Bob's books though it had to be pretended that it was Jonny who was getting him and not Anne.
He gave a good price . . . .

H.H.   5/5/73

Sorry to have been silent for so long. It has been rather a
time of despond. The worst one only happened yesterday

which was that Lucy had a baby (girl) in a London hospital &
there is something wrong with it but the doctors won't tell us
what until they have "discussed it with the parents" [The
baby very soon died] . . .

Eddie has been here for the last month. He comes down at
noon, goes back to bed immediately after lunch and comes
down again at 7 . . . He begins his serious drinking in the
evening. WHISKY. "Just another FINGER, my dear; perhaps
TWO fingers, my dear." They have become handfuls by
bedtime. But the thing is that, unlike most, it makes him
mellower and funnier, though it becomes a bit dangerous
when one has people to stay whom he doesn't know. Then he
is inclined to TRY to shock. . . .

N.M.   10/5/73

The baby, how too awful for you – one always thinks it is
the very worst thing that can happen . . .

Have you come in for a spot of Evelyn [his Diaries were
being serialised]? I see it incredibly late, long after anybody
else . . . He loved the bookshop, & as he destroyed the things
he loved, I daresay you'll come in for a bad time presently. . . .

N.M.   25/5/73

I think I am dying. There's not much evidence exc: the
doctor says she must have everything that she wants, & I'm
getting the one thing I do want, a new nurse, tomorrow. Oh
the jokes we could have had about this one if you & Anne had
been there . . .

Debo came & we had shrieks as you may imagine over the
WILL . . . Better stop. I'll try again. [For the first & only time
there is no "Love from Nancy"]

H.H. 31/5/73

. . . There was a letter from you this morning which brought on floods from us both. There was also a letter from Lucy which I shan't tell you about except that there was further flooding . . .

Anne sends much love. So do I.

EPILOGUE

Nancy Mitford died on 30 June 1973, and her funeral took place at Swinbrook on 7 July. Both the Hills and the Buchanans assumed that the other couple would go to the funeral, and neither was there. The following Monday, Lady Pamela Berry, who knew the shop well, arrived like a tornado; she rebuked Handy for his non-appearance, telling him it was outrageous that he had not closed the shop in Nancy's memory. It was a sad misunderstanding.

Heywood Hill died in 1986, two years after Handy Buchanan. Both their widows, Anne and Mollie, are still alive as I write.

For those who know the bookshop, these letters will be a reminder of a previous generation. For those who have not dealt with us, perhaps never heard of us, we are still very much in business, independent as ever and proud of our survival.

Writings by NANCY MITFORD

1931   *Highland Fling*

1932   *Christmas Pudding*

1935   *Wigs on the Green*

1938   *The Ladies of Alderley* (ed.)

1939   *The Stanleys of Alderley* (ed.)

1940   *Pigeon Pie*

1945   *The Pursuit of Love*

1949   *Love in a Cold Climate*

1950   *The Princesse de Clèves* by the Countess de
        La Fayette (trans.)

1951   *The Blessing*

1951   *The Little Hut* by André Roussin (trans.)

1954   *Madame de Pompadour*

1955   "The English Aristocracy"

1956   *Noblesse Oblige* by Alan Ross et al (ed.)

1957   *Voltaire in Love*

1960   *Don't Tell Alfred*

1962   *The Water Beetle*

1966   *The Sun King*

1970   *Frederick the Great*

1986   *A Talent to Annoy: Essays, Journalism and
        Reviews 1929–1968*, ed. Charlotte Mosley

1993   *Love from Nancy: The Letters of Nancy Mitford*,
        ed. Charlotte Mosley

1996   *The Letters of Nancy Mitford and Evelyn Waugh*,
        ed. Charlotte Mosley

ACKNOWLEDGEMENTS

Nancy's letters to Heywood are with the Hill archive in the Lilly Library, Bloomington, Indiana; I am very grateful to their librarians for permission to quote from them. Photocopies of them are kept in the (much fuller) Chatsworth archive, which also contain Heywood's letters to Nancy. I have had constant access there and could not have completed this book without the welcome and encouragement of the late Duke and the Dowager Duchess of Devonshire and their secretary Helen Marchant.

Those who know the bookshop will realise how much I owe to the technical skills and help of my colleagues, particularly Kirsty Anderson and Venetia Vyvyan who had to decipher my handwriting.

The photographs come from albums belonging to Nancy's and Heywood's families. Lady Anne Hill and her daughter Harriet have given their help and support, for which I am properly grateful.

My thanks also to James Fergusson for his brilliant work on footnotes, and to my publisher John Nicoll and editor Jane Havell for their enthusiasm and professionalism.

I could not have completed the editing without the love and understanding of my wife Laura.

John Saumarez Smith
June 2004

BIOGRAPHICAL INDEX

Bob	Hon. Robert Gathorne-Hardy
Captain	Cyril Connolly
Colonel	Gaston Palewski
Crafty	Handasyde Buchanan
Debo	Duchess of Devonshire
Decca	Hon. Jessica Treuhaft
Eddie	Hon. Edward Gathorne-Hardy
Handy	Handasyde Buchanan
Jamie	Hamish Hamilton
Jonny	Jonathan Gathorne-Hardy
Miss Liz	Elizabeth Forbes
Woman	Hon. Pamela Jackson

ACTON, Sir Harold (1904–94). Biographer, autobiographer and novelist. Owner of La Pietra, outside Florence, where he frequently entertained his literary friends from England. N.M.'s first biographer, an exact contemporary of hers and a close friend.

BUCHANAN, Handasyde (1907–84). Bookseller and bibliographer. He worked for Michael Williams at 3 Curzon Street from 1930 to 1940, and was invited to join Heywood Hill's in 1945. After H.H.'s retirement in 1965, he ran the shop until 1974.

BUCHANAN, Mollie (b. 1909) née Catleugh, then Friese-Green. Came to Heywood Hill's in 1943 and helped to keep it going with N.M. in wartime. Married *Handasyde Buchanan* in 1949; managed the shop accounts until 1972 when she retired.

CRANBROOK, Dorothy, Dowager Countess of (1879–1968). Lady Anne Hill's mother. Her sons were John (1900–78), the 4th Earl, known as Jock, who married Fidelity Seebohm; *Eddie Gathorne-Hardy*, *Bob Gathorne-Hardy* and Antony Gathorne-Hardy (1907–76). She lived at Snape Priory, near Saxmundham, Suffolk, to which H.H. and Anne moved after his retirement.

DEVONSHIRE, Duchess of (b. 1920). Sixth Mitford sister and the only surviving one, Deborah. Married Lord Andrew Cavendish in 1941; he became the 11th Duke of Devonshire in 1950. Author of *The House* (1982), *The Estate* (1990), *The Garden at Chatsworth* (1999) and others. Mother of Emma, Peregrine ("Stoker", the Marquess of Hartington, who succeeded his father as the 12th Duke of Devonshire in 2004) and Sophie.

FORBES, Elizabeth (b. 1924). Bookseller. Went to Heywood Hill's in 1946 and retired in 1972 to become an opera critic. Author of *Mario and Grisi*, 1985.

GATHORNE-HARDY, Hon. Edward (1901–78). *Anne Hill's* second brother and old friend of N.M. Worked for Elkin Mathews after Oxford University, later for the British Council in Athens, Cyprus and Cairo. Retired to Athens. Very widely read, he compiled *Inadvertencies*, a collection of doubles-entendres in literature.

GATHORNE-HARDY, Jonathan (b. 1933). Writer, son of Antony Gathorne-Hardy. After Eton, he briefly worked at Heywood Hill's, then combined copy-writing with being a novelist; author of books on English public schools, the British nanny, Gerald Brenan and others.

GATHORNE-HARDY, Hon. Robert (1902–73). Writer and owner of Mill House Press, Stanford Dingley. *Anne Hill*'s third brother, he also worked for Elkin Mathews. Biographer of Logan Pearsall Smith and editor of the diaries of Lady Ottoline Morrell.

GILMOUR, Geoffrey (d. 1981). Connoisseur and collector. Close friend of N.M. and H.H., he lived in rue du Bac, Paris, in considerable style. Both correspondents sometimes referred to him as Jefferson Cohen, for his frequent absences in Switzerland "doubtless counting his money"; after a story that involved his swinging from a chandelier, they lost no opportunity to play on jokes about swinging.

HAMILTON, Hamish (1900–87). One of the leading publishers of his generation, called "Prefect of London publishers and perfect pal" by *Harold Acton*. Close friend of N.M. who could be critical of his taste and business methods.

HILL, Lady Anne (b. 1912). Née Gathorne-Hardy, married H.H. in 1938. Worked in the bookshop until 1943, then had two daughters, *Harriet Hill* and *Lucy Hill*. Author of *Trelawny's Strange Relations*, 1956.

HILL, Derek (1918–2000). Artist. Younger brother of *John Hill*. N.M. sometimes referred to him as Maître. When asked by *Jonathan Gathorne-Hardy* why he qualified to attend a shop party celebrating the first 50 years, reserved for those who had worked there, he said that he had worked for Heywood Hill's every day since it opened in 1936. Claimed to have taught the art of watercolour painting to H.R.H. The Prince of Wales.

HILL, Harriet (b. 1943). Daughter of H.H. and Anne Hill. Married first the artist Tim Behrens in 1963 and had three children; then Simon Frazer. She founded Memorials by Artists after the death of her step-daughter Sophie in 1985.

HILL, John and Sheila. Sister and brother-in-law of H.H. Parents of Jo, Nick, Heywood and Rod. For many years John Hill ran Green and Abbott, interior decorators.

HILL, Lucy (b. 1946). Daughter of H.H. and Anne Hill. Married Geordie Redpath in 1970; five children.

JACKSON, Hon. Pamela (1907–94). Second of the Mitford sisters, she was married to Professor Derek Jackson from 1936 to 1951. Non-political and unsocial, she was N.M.'s favourite nurse in the years of her illness.

JEBB, Cynthia (1898–1990). Née Noble, she married Gladwyn Jebb (later Lord Gladwyn) in 1929; he became Ambassador to France in 1954, serving there until 1960. Their English home was at Bramfield, within easy distance of the Hills in Sussex. Her son Miles edited her diaries in 1995.

LEES-MILNE, James (1908–97). Biographer and diarist. Close friend of N.M. and H.H. for most of his life. After N.M.'s funeral, which he described brilliantly in *Ancient as the Hills*, he was invited by Hamish Hamilton to write her biography; his diary records his reasons for refusing. He married Alvilde (née Bridges) in 1951, whose first husband had been Viscount Chaplin; she was a gardener and garden writer.

MOSLEY, Hon. Lady (1910–2003). Diana, third of the Mitford sisters. She married first Bryan Guinness, then in 1936 Sir Oswald Mosley. Author of *A Life of Contrasts* and others.

TREUHAFT, Hon. Jessica (1917–96). Fifth of the Mitford sisters and natural rebel. She married first Esmond Romilly (died 1941), then Robert Treuhaft. Author of *Hons and Rebels* (1960), *A Fine Old Conflict* (1977) and others.

INDEX